CIVIL WAR LEADERS

ESSENTIAL LIBRARY OF
★ THE CIVIL ★
WAR

BY JUDY DODGE CUMMINGS

CONTENT CONSULTANT

MATT GALLMAN, PHD
DEPARTMENT OF HISTORY
UNIVERSITY OF FLORIDA

Essential Library

An Imprint of Abdo Publishing
abdopublishing.com

abdopublishing.com

Published by Abdo Publishing, a division of ABDO, PO Box 398166, Minneapolis, Minnesota 55439. Copyright © 2017 by Abdo Consulting Group, Inc. International copyrights reserved in all countries. No part of this book may be reproduced in any form without written permission from the publisher. Essential Library™ is a trademark and logo of Abdo Publishing.

Printed in the United States of America, North Mankato, Minnesota

052016
092016

THIS BOOK CONTAINS
RECYCLED MATERIALS

Cover Photos: Julian Vannerson/Library of Congress, left; Mathew Brady/US National Archives and Records Administration, middle left; Library of Congress, middle right, right
Interior Photos: Julian Vannerson/Library of Congress, 1 (left); Mathew Brady/US National Archives and Records Administration, 1 (middle left); Library of Congress, 1 (middle right), 1 (right), 10, 37, 42, 53; Corbis, 4, 28, 45, 64; Currier & Ives/Library of Congress, 7, 13; Everett Historical/Shutterstock Images, 14, 17, 46, 84, 94, 98 (left), 98 (right); Alexander Gardner/Library of Congress, 19; Bingham & Dodd/Library of Congress, 25; Anthony Berger/Library of Congress, 27; Mathew Brady/Library of Congress, 31, 99 (top); Bettmann/Corbis, 33; Red Line Editorial, 35; Henry Alexander Ogden/Library of Congress, 49, 71; Don Troiani/Corbis, 51; Mathew Brady/Buyenlarge/Getty Images, 54; Frederick Gutekunst/Library of Congress, 57, 99 (bottom); US National Park Service, 59; S. T. Blessing/Library of Congress, 68; Henszey & Co./Library of Congress, 73; AS400 DB/Corbis, 74, 77; Sam A. Cooley/Library of Congress, 83; Timothy H. O'Sullivan/ Library of Congress, 86; Silsbee, Case & Co./Library of Congress, 89

Editor: Susan Bradley
Series Designers: Kelsey Oseid and Maggie Villaume

Cataloging-in-Publication Data

Names: Cummings, Judy Dodge, author.
Title: Civil War leaders / by Judy Dodge Cummings.
Description: Minneapolis, MN : Abdo Publishing, [2017] | Series: Essential library
    of the Civil War | Includes bibliographical references and index.
Identifiers: LCCN 2015960307 | ISBN 9781680782769 (lib. bdg.) |
    ISBN 9781680774658 (ebook)
Subjects: LCSH: United States--History--Civil War, 1861-1865--Juvenile
    literature. | Generals--Confederate States of America--History--19th century--
    Juvenile literature. | Soldiers--Confederate States of America--History--19th
    century--Juvenile literature.
Classification: DDC 973.7--dc23
LC record available at http://lccn.loc.gov/2015960307

CONTENTS

The two-story Wigwam was a temporary wooden structure built by Chicago business leaders to host the 1860 Republican National Convention.

CHAPTER

★ 1 ★

DUELING REPUBLICS

On May 16, 1860, delegates poured into Chicago, Illinois, for the Republican National Convention. This gathering to nominate a candidate for president met in the Wigwam, a barnlike building that held 12,000 people. State delegates sat on the stage, supporters crammed the floor below, and spectators crowded into the aisles and gallery.

The Republican Party was only six years old. Abolitionists had founded this political organization to halt the spread of slavery into the western territories. Tensions over slavery had already divided Northerners and Southerners in the Democratic Party. That split meant a Republican had a chance to win the US presidency in the November election.

THE NEW REPUBLICAN PRESIDENT

Supporters of William H. Seward, the radical abolitionist from New York, thought they had the nomination locked up. However, backers of Abraham Lincoln, the moderate former congressman from Illinois, packed the hall and were making deals. By custom, candidates did not appear in person at the convention. Supporters of both Lincoln and Seward worked feverishly to convince delegates from key states to commit votes to their candidate. Lincoln backers whispered Southerners would never vote for Seward in the general election. His views on slavery were too extreme. Lincoln opposed slavery, but he had promised not to uproot it in states where it already existed. Lincoln, supporters promised, was the man who could deliver the presidency to the Republican Party.

The crowd in the Wigwam was fired up. When Michigan delegates seconded the nomination of Seward, the New Yorkers jumped to their feet and cheered so loudly the rafters trembled. When Ohio delegates seconded Lincoln's nomination, one spectator said the noise was louder than "a thousand steam whistles [and] ten acres of hotel gongs."[1]

After the first round of voting, Seward was ahead. But on the second ballot, Lincoln closed to within four votes. The Ohio delegation had its own candidate in the running—Salmon Chase. Chase, Ohio's former US senator and governor, did not stand a chance of winning the nomination, but the Ohio delegates would not relinquish their block of votes without getting something in return. Just before the third ballot was cast, a Lincoln supporter whispered to an Ohio delegate: if Ohio threw its votes to Lincoln and Lincoln won the presidency, Salmon Chase could have "anything he wants."[2] Four Ohio delegates switched their votes to Lincoln. The ballots were counted and the Wigwam exploded. Lincoln was the Republican nominee for president of the United States.

In the campaign that followed, Lincoln repeated his pledge not to interfere with slavery in states where it already existed.

Abraham Lincoln's rugged facial features and exceptionally long limbs caused many to make fun of his ungainly appearance.

Southerners did not believe him, but because the Democratic Party had split over the issue of slavery, proslavery factions could not rally enough support behind one candidate. On November 6, 1860, Abraham Lincoln was elected president. Even before the results were announced, states of the Deep South prepared to secede from the United States.

THE PRESIDENT OF THE NEW REPUBLIC

South Carolina was the first state to go. On December 20, 1860, its representatives voted to secede, and they called for other Southern states to hold a convention to create a new national government. When this convention met on February 4, 1861, Mississippi, Florida, Alabama, Georgia, and Louisiana had already seceded, with Texas soon to follow.

On the afternoon of February 10, 1861, Jefferson and Varina Davis were pruning rosebushes in the garden of their Mississippi plantation. A slave handed Mr. Davis a telegram. As he read silently, his wife said, "He looked so grieved that I feared some evil had befallen our family."[3] Perhaps Davis looked stricken because his distinguished career in the US government had just ended. The telegram informed Davis that delegates from the seceding states had chosen him to be president of the Confederate States of America.

Davis was inaugurated on February 18, 1861. He used the Declaration of Independence to justify secession. If the government harms the people it was created to protect, then the people have the right to abolish that government, he asserted. The new Confederate vice president, Alexander Stephens, was blunter. He said the Confederacy was founded on the principle that "the Negro is not equal to the white man."[4] The crowd at the inauguration cheered.

GUNS OF WAR

March 4, 1861, was cold and blustery in Washington, DC, when Abraham Lincoln was inaugurated. Cannons guarded the grounds of the unfinished capitol, and sharpshooters lined the roofs of nearby buildings. A tense crowd listened as Lincoln reaffirmed his pledge to not interfere with slavery. He also stated that secession was unconstitutional, and he was legally bound to "hold, occupy or possess" government property.[5] However, Lincoln vowed not to strike the first blow. "The government will not assail you," he told Southerners. "You can have no conflict without being yourselves the aggressors."[6] Lincoln believed the secession crisis was directed by a small, elite group of Southern planters. He was confident that if he took a firm but calm stance, no more slave states would

By the time Lincoln was inaugurated on March 4, 1861, seven of the nation's 34 states had seceded from the union over the issues of slavery and states' rights. The Confederate States of America would eventually consist of 11 states.

stampede out of the Union. But soon enough, the developing crisis at Fort Sumter caused Lincoln to realize he had misjudged Southern passions.

Control of Fort Sumter, the federal installation in the harbor of Charleston, South Carolina, became a test of wills between Lincoln and Davis. South

Carolina's leaders insisted the fort was their territory, and they demanded that federal troops vacate it. Lincoln refused. But federal troops inside the fort were running out of food, so Lincoln was forced to act. On April 6, 1861, he informed the governor of South Carolina he would send provisions to Fort Sumter, but he would not rearm the fort as long as it was not attacked. President Davis's response was swift and decisive. He ordered the Confederate commander in Charleston to destroy Fort Sumter if federal troops did not evacuate immediately. At midnight on April 12, the federal troops were given four hours to evacuate. As the clock ticked, neither side budged.

At 4:30 a.m. on April 12, the skies over Charleston Harbor lit up as a barrage of Confederate artillery fired on Fort Sumter. Thirty-six hours later, the federal commander inside the fort raised a white flag of surrender. The Civil War had begun. Although there were no combat deaths for either side, two Union soldiers died from an accidental artillery explosion during the 100-gun salute marking the Union's evacuation.

FRACTURED FRIENDSHIPS

Major Robert Anderson led the defense inside Fort Sumter. When Confederate messengers rowed out to tell him to surrender or the fort would be bombed, Anderson refused. The Confederate commander in Charleston who bombarded the fort was General P. G. T. Beauregard. Anderson had been Beauregard's artillery instructor at West Point Military Academy in New York. On the eve of the war, the US Army had only 17,000 men. Many of the officers knew each other personally. Now these friends would face each other in battle.[8]

Following the battle, Southerners were jubilant, while people in the North were furious. Lincoln called for 75,000 volunteers to suppress the rebellion.[9] Men from Massachusetts to Minnesota and everywhere in between swarmed to Washington, DC. Lincoln's call for an invading army pushed Arkansas, North Carolina, Tennessee, and Virginia to secede, and the Confederate government called for its own army of 100,000.[10] Both sides were convinced the war would be over in 90 days. Four grueling years and approximately 750,000 deaths later, leaders of both sides would finally order the guns to be silenced.[11]

CONFEDERATE DISSENSION

Confederate leaders disagreed about whether to fire on Fort Sumter. Confederate secretary of state Robert Toombs warned, "It is suicide, murder, and will lose us every friend at the North." But other leaders believed such an act would unify the Confederacy and compel other slave states to secede. Virginia Congressman Roger Pryor told a Charleston crowd, "If you want us to join you, strike a blow!"[12]

Public outrage in the North over the Confederacy's bombardment of Fort Sumter

President Lincoln was convinced the Emancipation Proclamation was both morally correct and militarily advantageous.

THE GREAT EMANCIPATOR: ABRAHAM LINCOLN

On July 22, 1862, President Lincoln gathered his cabinet for what the members thought was a regular meeting. Lincoln first relaxed the men with humorous stories as was his custom, and then he dropped a bombshell. He had decided to free the slaves in the rebelling states. The document that would become Lincoln's Emancipation Proclamation nearly six months later would transform the war and lead to the end of slavery throughout the nation.

HUMBLE BEGINNINGS

The man who would go down in history as the "Great Emancipator" was born in a one-room log cabin in Hardin County, Kentucky, on February 12, 1809. Abraham Lincoln spent his youth in both Kentucky and Indiana plowing fields and splitting wood, but he was rarely seen without a book stuffed in his pocket. When he was 22, Lincoln moved to New Salem, Illinois, and then to Illinois' capital city, Springfield, six years later. After serving four terms in the Illinois state legislature, he was elected to the US Congress in 1846. Lincoln did not seek reelection in 1848 and returned to Springfield to practice law.

By the 1850s, tensions over slavery had reached a boiling point, and Lincoln decided to reenter politics. In 1858, he ran for the US Senate against the eloquent Democrat Stephen A. Douglas. Upon accepting his party's nomination for the Senate, Lincoln argued that "A house divided against itself cannot stand."[1] He believed the United States could not permanently survive as a nation that was half-slave and half-free. During the campaign, Lincoln and Douglas engaged in a series of seven debates across the state, and although Douglas won reelection to the Senate, Lincoln gained the national attention that would propel him to the White House only two years later.

COMMANDER IN CHIEF

Only weeks after being sworn in as president, Lincoln had to give his full attention to his new role as commander in chief. Nothing in his life had prepared him for the hard decisions he would face in this capacity. After the attack on Fort Sumter, there were fewer than 20,000 men in the US Army, and many officers had resigned to join the Confederate army. Lincoln needed a strategy, a commander, and thousands of troops.[2]

Lincoln's initial military strategy was known as the Anaconda Plan. Similar to the huge snake that slowly suffocates its prey, Lincoln aimed to strangle the Confederacy. To do this, he blockaded

As commander in chief, President Lincoln was intimately involved in formulating strategies that would help the Union win the war.

Southern ports and focused on seizing control of the Mississippi River in order to split the Confederacy. He was also determined to keep the proslavery border states of Missouri, Kentucky, Delaware, and Maryland from seceding and to prevent European nations from aiding the Confederacy.

Lincoln was confident one decisive victory would crush the Confederate rebellion. However, such a victory proved elusive, in part because Lincoln could not find the right commander. On July 16, 1861, General Irvin McDowell led approximately 35,000 Union soldiers into Virginia, only 32 miles (51 km) west of Washington, DC.[3] Their goal was to sever the railroad link at the town of Manassas and then march on the Confederate capital at Richmond. Confederate general Thomas Jackson, earning the nickname of "Stonewall," held the line against a Union assault, and the Confederates' war whoop sent federal troops into a retreat.[4] This conflict would come to be known as the First Battle of Bull Run by the Union, named for the small stream that ran alongside the Union camp. What the Union had expected to be a certain victory turned into a major defeat.

The defeat at Bull Run taught Lincoln two things: he needed a better general, and he needed to learn military strategy. Lincoln checked out books from the Library of Congress and educated himself on military campaigns and army structure. At this time in history, armies focused on capturing key towns and cities, but Lincoln believed this approach was too time-consuming. He ordered

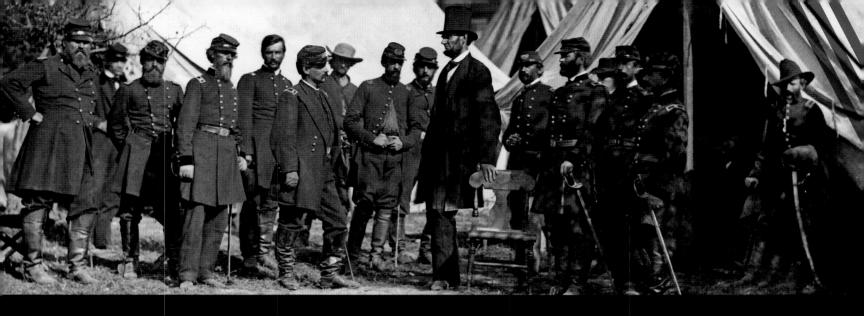

To President Lincoln's great dismay, he and General McClellan held widely differing views on what it would take for the Union to win the war.

his generals to ignore Confederate cities and instead crush the Confederate armies in the field.

In July 1861, Lincoln appointed General George McClellan to lead the main Union army, called the Army of the Potomac. On November 1, McClellan was promoted to general-in-chief of the entire Union army. When Lincoln explained the immensity of the task, McClellan exuded confidence. "I can do it all," he boasted.[5] Although McClellan's Peninsula Campaign included the intent to attack Richmond by land and water, he made very slow progress toward this goal. For months, Lincoln pressed McClellan to attack the enemy. For months, McClellan made excuses. Lincoln replaced McClellan with General John Pope as general-in-chief, leaving McClellan to command only the Army of the Potomac. But after federal troops were defeated at Bull Run for a second time in August 1862, Lincoln's options were limited. He reinstated McClellan as top commander, reluctantly telling his cabinet, "We must use the tools we have."[6]

McClellan finally engaged the Confederate army on September 17, 1862, after Confederate general Robert E. Lee invaded Maryland. The ensuing Battle of Antietam was the bloodiest day in US history. McClellan forced Lee to retreat; however, he then failed to pursue the Confederates into Virginia. Lincoln visited McClellan at his camp, urging him to go on the offensive. The general came up with one excuse after another. In October 1862, when McClellan wired Lincoln that his horses were too tired to attack, the president replied by telegraph in a rare display of anger, asking how the horses could possibly be tired given they had done nothing since Antietam. Lincoln had had enough, and he promptly relieved McClellan of his duties.

An army must have soldiers, and Lincoln needed more men than were volunteering to serve. On March 3, 1863, Congress passed a law that required all able-bodied men aged 20 to 45 to register for the draft. Despite the new law, there were ways to evade the draft for those unwilling to fight. For $300, a man could buy his way out or could hire a substitute.[7] The draft—and the evading of it—was controversial, but Lincoln believed it was necessary. He said the United States faced an opponent who "drives every able-bodied man . . . into his ranks . . . as a butcher drives bullocks into a slaughter-pen."[8] Lincoln would make certain the Northern army always outnumbered the Confederates.

DEALING WITH DISSENT

The quickest way to transport troops from Northern states to Washington, DC, was through the railroad hub in Baltimore, Maryland. Maryland had not seceded, but Baltimore seethed with Southern sympathizers. On April 19, 1861, federal soldiers arrived in Baltimore by train and were met by an angry, violent mob. Four soldiers and eleven rioters were killed.[9]

To quell any future trouble, Lincoln suspended habeas corpus in cases involving public safety. Habeas corpus is a rule that prevents the government from jailing people without due process. By suspending the need for a court order, Lincoln could lock up suspected Southern sympathizers without having

NORTHERN SUPPORTERS OF SLAVERY

Proslavery secret societies such as the Sons of Liberty and the Knights of the Golden Circle sprang up in the Union in 1863. These peace groups wanted to negotiate an end to the war. Most members of such groups were Northern Democrats, and opponents called them Copperheads after the venomous snake. When the leader of the Copperheads, Ohio congressman Clement Vallandigham, called on Union soldiers to desert, he was charged with treason and jailed. Democrats were enraged, but Lincoln had little sympathy. As commander in chief, he wondered why he "must not touch a hair of the wily agitator who induces [the soldiers] to desert?"[10] Nonetheless, Lincoln chose to release Vallandigham from jail and banish him to the Confederacy instead.

to prove their guilt at a trial, a move he deemed necessary to protect the Union. Roger Taney, the chief justice of the US Supreme Court, declared Lincoln's actions unconstitutional, but Lincoln, with Congress's later approval, continued the suspension of habeas corpus.

NEW YORK DRAFT RIOTS

On July 11, 1863, a list of draftees was posted in New York City alongside the names of 3,100 Union soldiers who had been killed at the Battle of Gettysburg less than two weeks earlier.[11] When a second drawing of draft numbers took place on July 13, a mob composed mostly of Irish Americans attacked the draft office and rioted across the city. Citizens were irate that rich young men could escape the draft for a fee of $300, while poor men were expected to fight. African Americans were specifically targeted by the agitated mob, as many in the crowd feared that free blacks and emancipated slaves from the South would take their jobs. A black church, a black orphanage, and black rooming houses were destroyed. More than 100 people died in four days of riots that finally ended when Union troops arrived in the city and reestablished order.[12]

SOLUTION TO SLAVERY

As a man, Lincoln was morally opposed to slavery, but when the war began, Lincoln insisted his only goal was to restore the Union, not free the slaves. Escaped slaves who crossed Union lines were returned to their Southern masters. Lincoln had to reassess his objectives as the military situation continued to deteriorate in 1862. From June 25 to July 1, the Confederate army pushed federal troops from the outskirts of Richmond all the way back to Washington, DC. Wall Street panicked, causing stock values to plummet. Morale in the North sank, and many Union soldiers deserted.

Lincoln decided that as commander in chief, he needed help from wherever possible to win the war—including from African Americans. Escaped slaves would no longer be returned to their Southern masters, nor would black men be denied the right to join the Union army. On September 22, 1862, Lincoln announced that as of New Year's Day 1863, all people held in bondage in a rebelling state "shall be then, thenceforth, and forever free."[13]

This declaration, known as the Emancipation Proclamation, set off an immediate and intense reaction. Confederate President Jefferson Davis called the proclamation the most appalling act "recorded in the history of guilty man."[14] General McClellan condemned it as a statement intended to provoke slave insurrection in the South. Lincoln, however, was confident he had done the right thing. He stated upon signing the document, "If my name ever goes into history it will be for this act, and my whole soul is in it."[15]

Although Lincoln could not actually liberate slaves in territory held by the Confederate army, the Emancipation Proclamation had practical implications for the war. France and the United Kingdom, two antislavery nations, decided not to aid the Confederacy after the proclamation was announced. The document also called for the military recruitment of African Americans. By the end of the war, close to 200,000 black troops would fight for the Union.[16] The Emancipation Proclamation transformed the Civil War from a conflict to preserve the status quo into a fight over slavery.

REELECTION

Since 1832, no US president had been elected to a second term, and Lincoln faced a challenging fight for reelection in 1864. Activists known as Radical Republicans from Lincoln's own party sought alternative candidates. The party ultimately decided to choose Lincoln, with the party platform supporting continuation of the war until the Confederacy surrendered unconditionally.

To bring Southern representation to the ticket, Senator Andrew Johnson, a Democrat from Tennessee, was nominated as vice president in place of the sitting vice president, Hannibal Hamlin of Maine. Concerned a future president might invalidate the Emancipation Proclamation, Lincoln insisted the party endorse a constitutional amendment to abolish slavery. Support for the proposed Thirteenth Amendment was added to the Republican platform.

The Democratic candidate for president was Lincoln's grumbling former general, George McClellan. McClellan ran a low-key campaign marked by very few public appearances. He was ineffective in uniting the fractured Democratic Party. Some members wanted an immediate end to the war; others wanted the war to end only after the Confederate states reentered the Union. McClellan tried to tread between the two camps. However, by the fall of 1864, the tide of war had turned in favor of the Union, and McClellan's support fell. On November 8, 1864, Lincoln won 55 percent of the popular vote to McClellan's 45 percent, as well as

Andrew Johnson was the only senator from a Confederate state who remained loyal to the Union.

22 of the 25 states.[17] Even in the midst of a civil war, the people had reelected Lincoln to end the brutal war and reconstruct the nation. No one realized he would not live long enough to finish both tasks.

CARTES DE VISITE

By the mid-1850s, cartes de visite, or visiting cards, were a fad. These 2.5 x 4-inch (6.4 x 10.2 cm) photos were exchanged the way children today exchange school photos or sports cards. People not only collected cartes de visite of friends and family but also of famous people, often storing their collection in albums made for that purpose.

The first carte de visite of Abraham Lincoln was made from a photograph taken in February 1860. Following a speech Lincoln gave at Cooper Union in New York, photographer Mathew Brady took his picture. Lincoln later claimed that "Brady and the Cooper Institute made me president."[18] Voters could more closely identify with Lincoln by seeing him in various poses, and even the state of his facial hair became a topic of public discussion. Prior to the 1860 election, a young girl from Westfield, New York, wrote to Lincoln suggesting that he grow a beard to cover his thin face. Lincoln took her advice and thanked her in person after his successful election.

During the war, President Lincoln's image could be found in almost every home album in the North. One popular photo featured an intimate family moment. In it, the president sits with an album on his lap and his son Tad stands beside him. The pair is looking down at the photo album. The viewer can imagine the conversation between Lincoln and his son as they page through the book. Images like this one helped cement a bond between the leader of the nation and his citizens.

Cartes de visite were inexpensive to make and were particularly popular with soldiers and their families during the war. Soldiers—and even presidents—liked having a remembrance of their loved ones when they were far from home.

Jefferson Davis was inaugurated as president of the Confederate States of America on February 18, 1861, in Montgomery, Alabama.

RELENTLESS REBEL: JEFFERSON DAVIS

On January 21, 1861, the United States Senate chamber was packed. One after another, five Southern senators rose and said their good-byes. Jefferson Davis of Mississippi spoke last. The thin man explained in a quiet voice why he felt compelled to follow his state out of the Union. "We but tread in the path of our fathers when we proclaim our independence. . . . This is done not in hostility to others . . . but from the high and solemn motive of defending and protecting the rights we inherited."[1] When Davis's speech ended, members of the Senate rose and watched silently as their five former colleagues departed the chamber and the nation.

ADVOCATE OF SLAVERY

Jefferson Davis was born in Kentucky on June 3, 1808. He grew up on a Mississippi cotton plantation, where slavery played a central role in his family's daily life. After graduating from West Point Military Academy in 1828, Davis fought in both the Black Hawk War (1832) and the Mexican–American War (1846–1848). He gained experience in military strategy and command in his role as secretary of war under President Franklin Pierce. Except for a brief stint as a congressman, most of Davis's legislative experience came from his years in the Senate. He was a senator from 1847 to 1851, and then he returned to the Senate in 1857 just as slavery threatened to tear apart the nation.

As a United States senator, Davis was an outspoken advocate for slavery. He believed that as long as masters treated their slaves humanely, there was nothing morally wrong with the institution. Slaves were property, and a man had a right to own property.

Davis shared the belief of many in the South that the future of the country hinged on the 1860 election. He disapproved of the radical, proslavery secessionists known as fire-eaters. However, when Lincoln was elected, Davis decided to follow the lead of his state. Mississippi seceded on January 9, 1861, and 12 days later, Davis resigned from the Senate.

On February 18, 1861, Davis was sworn in as president of the Confederate States of America. In his inauguration speech, Davis addressed both the North and the South. "A reunion with the States from which we have separated is neither practicable nor desirable."[2] Davis was making it clear: the Southern states had seceded and would not return to the United States.

GOVERNMENT ON THE FLY

As president of the Confederacy, Davis had a colossal task. He was trying to win a war while governing a nation composed of 11 independently minded states that

Davis had chronic inflammation in his left eye, so many of his photos were taken in right profile to conceal it.

were suspicious of central government. In addition, in its infancy, the nation had limited financial and material resources aside from those that were voluntarily—and unpredictably—contributed by its states and citizens. Such a job required the skills of a master politician, and Davis was not one. The art of compromise eluded him. Tensions between Davis and his cabinet created an unstable government throughout the war.

In the winter of 1861, Davis worked quickly and efficiently to prepare for war. He helped draft a new constitution, appointed a cabinet, outfitted an army, stockpiled guns and ammunition, and sent a team of representatives to the United Kingdom to negotiate an alliance. In an effort to please politicians across the Confederacy, he appointed a representative from each state to a cabinet position. This resulted in a group of men with explosive personalities, all driven by their own agendas and by pressure from others who had their own interests.

Davis did not take disagreement well; he interpreted it as criticism and usually ignored it. Within a month of taking office, Davis split with his vice

A SICK PRESIDENCY

Illness plagued Davis throughout his presidency. He suffered from herpes in his left eye, recurring malaria, nerve pain, and insomnia. All these conditions were made worse by stress. After the Confederate defeats at Gettysburg and Vicksburg, Davis was confined to his bed for weeks, and his physician was convinced the president was near death. Davis spent several months of his four-year presidency incapacitated, and his poor health crippled his effectiveness as a political leader.

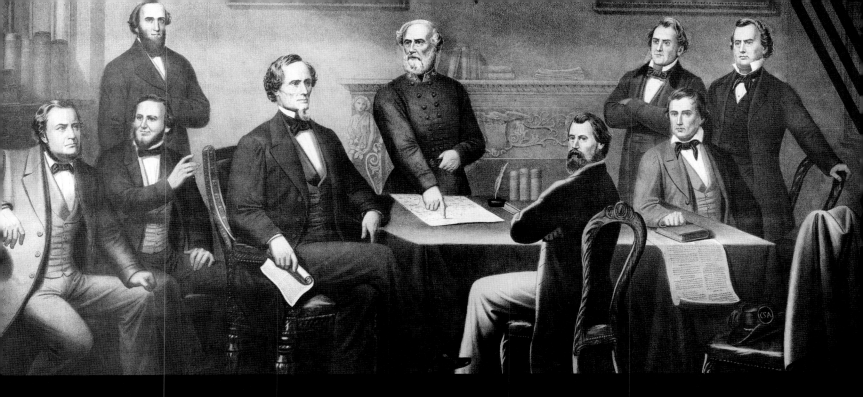

President Davis formed a cabinet of advisers but seldom took their advice. He treated disagreement with his views as a sign of disloyalty to the Confederate cause.

president, Alexander Stephens of Georgia. Like Lincoln, Davis instituted a military draft and suspended habeas corpus, actions Stephens loudly opposed. Stephens publicly criticized Davis, calling him "weak, vacillating, timid, petulant, peevish, [and] obstinate."[3]

Other cabinet officials complained Davis ruled like a dictator. The first secretary of war, LeRoy Pope Walker, was excluded from military decisions. Davis sent between six and twelve telegrams a day to his generals on the field, often without any input from Walker. Davis also seemed unable to delegate work to subordinates. One day a clerk counted 1,500 letters, memos, and orders on Davis's desk. Davis's micromanagement caused rapid turnover in the cabinet. During the life of the Confederacy there would be six secretaries of war, three secretaries of state, three attorneys general, and two treasury secretaries.

DEFENDING THE NATION

When the war began, the Confederate States of America stretched from the Atlantic Ocean in the east to Texas in the west. In order to defend this vast terrain, Davis issued two controversial orders in 1862: all enlistments would last until the war ended, and all able-bodied white men aged 18 to 35 were subject to the draft. What irritated some people was that if a man owned at least 20 slaves, he was exempt from the draft, causing many to complain that poor men were fighting to protect the interests of rich men. Some people felt Davis was acting like a tyrant, and about half of the men eligible for the draft failed to sign up.

Davis's critics said he played favorites when appointing generals. He passed over capable men who were not his friends or acquaintances from his time in the army. Anyone who criticized Davis's military strategy suffered consequences. When General Beauregard wrote a report that accused Davis of preventing him from pursuing the defeated Union army after the Confederate victory at Manassas (referred to by the Union as Bull Run), Davis sought revenge. He called

BRITISH NORTH AMERICA

Oregon

Washington
Territory

Nevada
Territory

Utah
Territory

California

New Mexico
Territory

Dakota Territory

Nebraska Territory

Colorado
Territory

Kansas

Indian
Territory

Texas

Minnesota

Michigan

Wisconsin

Iowa

Illinois

Missouri

Arkansas

Louisiana

New Hampshire
Vermont

Maine

New York

Massachusetts

Rhode
Island
Connecticut

Pennsylvania

New Jersey

Delaware
Maryland

Ohio

Indiana

West
Virginia

Virginia

Kentucky

Tennessee

North Carolina

South
Carolina

Georgia

Alabama

Mississippi

Florida

Pacific

Ocean

Atlantic

Ocean

THE BAHAMAS

Gulf of Mexico

MEXICO

Union states without slavery

Union states and regions with slavery

Confederate states

Territories

The Davis administration faced a monumental challenge in trying to defend the far-reaching Confederate territory. Both soldiers and material resources were hard to come by for the new nation.

Beauregard a liar, ridiculed him frequently, and blocked him from command positions later in the war even though Beauregard could have helped the Confederate cause.

The two generals Davis valued the most were Robert E. Lee and Albert Sidney Johnston. Johnston was given command in the west, but he was killed at the Battle of Shiloh in 1862. From then on, Davis put his greatest trust in Lee, whom he appointed to lead the Army of Northern Virginia. The two men had a close relationship, mostly because Lee knew how to handle Davis's eccentricities. Lee always replied quickly to Davis's telegrams or letters, a task most generals in the field found tedious. After the war, Lee defended Davis, saying, "Few people could have done better than Mr. Davis."[4]

IRREPARABLE LOSS

General Albert Sidney Johnston launched a surprise attack on General Grant's 40,000-man army at Shiloh, Tennessee, on April 6, 1862. Victory seemed within Johnston's grasp. However, when federal troops held tight to a patch of sunken road, the Confederate advance stalled. Johnston confidently shouted to his men, "I will lead you."[5] As he led a charge, a musket ball struck Johnston in the rear of his leg, severing an artery. His boot filled with blood, and he died before his men could locate the wound. When President Davis learned of Johnston's death, he said, "Our loss is irreparable."[6]

TROUBLE ON THE HOME FRONT

As the war dragged into its third year, Davis had to deal with angry citizens. The Confederate Congress taxed personal property, but it exempted slaves when calculating property, thus benefiting large plantation owners. All farms, regardless of size, had to give 10 percent of their produce to the government. This angered small farmers who did not have a large slave labor force to help them till or

At the time of his death in April 1862, General Albert Sidney Johnston was highly regarded by President Davis and was considered by many to be the Confederacy's finest commander.

harvest their fields. The Confederate army was authorized to seize crops and livestock and then reimburse farmers with Confederate money, but this money was not worth the paper it was printed on. Many farmers stopped selling their crops, and some stopped growing crops altogether.

When supplies of goods are low but demand remains high, prices go up. Davis did not pay attention to the economic troubles brewing in the Confederacy, and by 1863 inflation had skyrocketed. Between late 1862 and early 1865, for example, the price of a barrel of flour in North Carolina rose 2,800 percent.[7] The citizens revolted. On April 2, 1863, the women of Richmond rioted to protest the high prices, smashing windows and looting stores. When Davis heard the commotion, he raced into the street. He threw a handful of coins into a crowd of angry women, yelling at them that it was all that he had. Then Davis gave the women five minutes to leave, after which he would order the troops to open fire. The rioters went home, and morale throughout the Confederacy sagged.

CONSPIRACIES BOTH NORTH AND SOUTH

On February 28, 1864, General Hugh Kilpatrick led a raid on Richmond to free Union prisoners. Details of the raid were leaked, and Confederates ambushed the invaders. Documents found on the corpse of Union colonel Ulric Dalgren revealed the raiders had intended to kill Davis and the Confederate cabinet. In the fall of 1864, Southern actor John Wilkes Booth began conspiring with several others to kidnap President Lincoln, whom he hated with a passion. On March 17, 1865, Booth stopped a carriage in which he expected to find Lincoln, only to find the president had changed his plans. The kidnapping plot was foiled, but Booth would try again.

EMANCIPATION

When President Lincoln authorized the recruitment of black soldiers as part of the Emancipation Proclamation, President Davis said the North was encouraging

SPIES IN THE HEART OF THE CONFEDERACY

Mary Bowser was a slave of John Van Lew, a wealthy Richmond businessman. When Van Lew died in 1843, his wife and children freed the family slaves but kept them on as paid servants. Van Lew's daughter, Elizabeth, a fervent abolitionist, used a large portion of her inheritance to purchase and then free relatives of the family's servants. Elizabeth went on to become a Union spy, and she enlisted Mary Bowser's help with spying when the war began. Bowser worked undercover as a servant for Davis. As she went about her work, Bowser, who had a photographic memory, eavesdropped on conversations and read Confederate war dispatches. This information was conveyed to Elizabeth Van Lew, who then passed it on to Union military intelligence. President Davis knew there was an information leak in his mansion, but suspicion never fell on Bowser until the war was nearly over.

"several millions of human beings of an inferior race, peaceful and contented laborers . . . to a general assassination of their masters."[8] The Confederate Congress later decreed any black person, slave or free, who was captured with weapons was to be tried for inciting a slave rebellion and was subject to the death penalty. However, as the Confederate army shrank in size, Davis was forced to rethink this policy.

On November 7, 1864, in one of the great ironies of history, Davis stood before the Confederate Congress and said it might be necessary to enlist slaves in the ranks of the Confederate army. This about-face was a military necessity, as the Union army had achieved multiple successes on the battlefield, and both soldiers and food were in short supply in the South. The Confederate Congress

MEDICAL MATRON

Phoebe Yates Pember was the chief administrator at Chimborazo Hospital in Richmond, reportedly the world's largest military hospital in its day. A law passed by the Confederacy in September 1862 commissioned women to serve as hospital matrons so that able-bodied men could take to the battlefield. It was Pember's responsibility to acquire and distribute all food and supplies for her patients. One of her toughest battles was guarding medicinal whiskey from the male staff. Pember spent much time consoling the dying. In her memoir, she described how she kept a patient alive by holding her finger over a severed artery on his hip. When the patient, who knew his condition was hopeless, directed Pember to remove her finger, he died.

authorized the plan in March 1865, but only a few dozen slaves joined the Confederate army before the war ended the following month.

NEVER QUIT

In the spring of 1865, Davis clung to the unrealistic belief that a Confederate victory was possible. All signs pointed to the opposite outcome. Half of the Southern army had deserted. General Lee informed Davis the Confederate army was failing. Vice President Stephens pursued a peace treaty with President Lincoln, but Lincoln said peace would come when the Confederate army disbanded and the South abolished slavery. Davis vowed to fight on.

Soon matters were taken out of his hands. On April 2, 1865, Davis was attending church in Richmond when he was handed a message. A gray pallor spread across his face as he read it. The Union army was just outside the city, and

General Lee could no longer defend the Confederate capital. Davis and his cabinet fled Richmond by train.

On April 4, from the government's new headquarters in Danville, Virginia, Davis urged his countrymen not to quit. He proposed a campaign of guerrilla warfare. He called on the citizens of the South to "meet the foe with fresh defiance, with unconquered and unconquerable hearts."[9] But Davis was not commanding soldiers on the field; General Lee was. Lee rejected the idea of a guerrilla war, and on April 9, he surrendered his army to General Ulysses S. Grant. This surrender was the death knell of the Confederacy. As the Civil War drew to a close, Jefferson Davis went into hiding. He was now a fugitive—a man wanted for treason against the United States of America.

DAVIS'S SENATE SUCCESSOR

On February 25, 1870, Hiram Rhodes Revels was sworn in as the first African-American member of Congress in American history when he became a senator from Mississippi. Jefferson Davis had held the office prior to Mississippi's secession from the Union. In debate prior to the ceremony, a senator from Maryland argued that Revels could not be a senator because he had not been a citizen for the nine years required by the Constitution. African Americans were not legally considered citizens until the Fourteenth Amendment was ratified on July 9, 1868. This senator's objections were overruled, and when Revels took the oath, spectators in the gallery rose and watched the dignified senator in silence.

General Robert E. Lee, *right of center with white beard*, was highly respected by his fellow commanders for his exceptional military capabilities.

THE MARBLE MODEL: ROBERT E. LEE

On April 17, 1861, Virginia seceded from the United States. The next day, President Lincoln offered General Robert E. Lee command of the Union army. Lee turned him down immediately, insisting he could never draw a sword against his home state of Virginia. For the following two days, Lee engaged in what his wife called "the severest struggle of his life."[1] He paced in the garden of his home at Arlington, Virginia, and prayed on his knees before bed. By the evening of the second day, Lee had made a decision. He resigned from the US Army. Before the ink on his resignation was even dry, Lee had become a brigadier general in the Confederate army.

MILITARY MAN

Robert E. Lee was born into a wealthy family in Stratford, Virginia, on January 19, 1807. He attended West Point, graduating second in his class in 1829. Lee's classmates nicknamed him "Marble Model" because of his stellar academic performance and his excellent conduct.[2] As a member of the army's elite Corps of Engineers, Lee constructed coastal fortifications around the United States until the Mexican–American War broke out in 1846. During this conflict, he served under General Winfield Scott, who said Lee was the "very best soldier I ever saw in the field."[3]

As disagreements over slavery heated up in the 1850s, Lee struggled with where his duty lay—with his nation or with his state. Lee personally owned five slaves and managed many others whom his wife had inherited. Lee believed slavery was both morally and politically evil, but he felt slaves were better off in the United States than they would have been in Africa. Slavery, according to Lee, was a bitter medicine black people had to swallow in order to advance, and he believed abolition would come in due time.

Following Lincoln's election, Lee was torn. He believed secession was no different than launching a revolution against the nation, but he also condemned the "selfish and dictatorial bearing" he felt the North had toward the South.[4] Ultimately, Lee joined with his home state. If Virginia stayed in the Union, so would he. After Lincoln called for an army of volunteers to suppress the rebellion, Virginia seceded and Lee followed.

CONFEDERATE GENERAL

For the first year of the war, Lee was kept on the sidelines as a military adviser to President Davis. Then in May 1862, when General Joseph Johnston was seriously wounded in the Battle of Seven Pines, Lee was given a field command of what

Lee served in the US Army for three decades before siding with the Confederacy.

would eventually become the Army of Northern Virginia. When Lee took over, the Union's Army of the Potomac under General McClellan was on the banks of the Chickahominy River, only a few miles from Richmond. Many people feared the Union would soon overtake the capital and crush the Confederacy before it had really begun. Although Lee was outnumbered two to one, he decided to strike first.

Using his engineering background, Lee ordered massive earthworks dug around Richmond to protect it from Union weaponry. Tired of digging, Lee's troops nicknamed him "the King of Spades," but this strategy allowed Lee to leave a small

Lee's marriage to Mary Anna Randolph Custis made him caretaker of the Custis family mansion, Arlington House.

ARLINGTON: FROM MANSION TO MAUSOLEUM

When Virginia seceded from the Union, Mary Anna Custis Lee fled from the Lees' home, Arlington House. The Union army occupied the mansion, using trees around the estate for firewood. A freedman's village housing 1,500 former slaves was built on the grounds, featuring a school, churches, stores, and a hospital. In 1864, a portion of the property became a national cemetery that is still in use today. After the war, Lee's son, Custis, sued the US government for compensation. After years in court, the federal government finally agreed to purchase the estate. On March 31, 1883, Custis Lee signed the transfer of title to the property. The person who accepted the deed to the estate was US Secretary of War Robert Todd Lincoln, son of the slain president.

force to defend the city while he used the bulk of his army to assault McClellan's right flank.[5] Over the course of seven days, Lee divided his army and struck the federal troops aggressively and repeatedly. McClellan abandoned his plan to take Richmond and retreated all the way down the Virginia Peninsula. The Seven Days Battles cemented Lee's reputation in both the South and the North as a sharp military strategist.

Lee's leadership of the Army of Northern Virginia revealed both his strengths and weaknesses as a commander. He used both offensive and defensive strategies effectively and creatively. The large entrenchments Lee ordered dug around Richmond were rare at this time in history, but they proved effective. Although stoic and calm off the battlefield, Lee had an intense combat instinct and was relentless in his assaults. During the Battle of Gaines' Mill, part of the Seven Days Battles, the rebel army suffered 9,000 casualties in six hours.[6] Still, Lee pressed on.

Lee believed several swift, significant victories would bring Lincoln to the negotiating table. Following a decisive Confederate victory at the Second Battle of Bull Run in August 1862, he convinced President Davis it was time to take the war into the North. On September 4, 1862, the Army of Northern Virginia crossed the Potomac River into Maryland. Lee hoped an invasion would undermine Northern morale, gain international recognition for the Confederacy, and increase the chances of pro-peace candidates succeeding in the North's November elections.

Upon arriving in Maryland, Lee made the controversial decision to divide his already depleted army. He sent General Stonewall Jackson with a portion of the troops to Harpers Ferry, Virginia, where there was a garrison of federal troops. This was a risky move because the Confederates were vastly outnumbered, but Lee knew General McClellan was a cautious, slow-moving leader. What Lee did not know was that a Union soldier had found a copy of Lee's battle plans in a field recently occupied by the rebels. Tipped off about Lee's moves, McClellan attacked the Confederates on September 17 along Antietam Creek near the town of Sharpsburg, Maryland.

"STONEWALL" JACKSON

1824–1863

During the First Battle of Bull Run, Confederate lieutenant general Thomas Jonathan Jackson earned his nickname. When a Union victory seemed imminent, Jackson rode in front of the line, urging his men to keep up the fight. As Brigadier General Barnard Bee's Confederate troops began to retreat, Bee hollered, "Look, men, there stands Jackson like a stone wall! Rally behind the Virginians."[7] Rally they did. The South won that battle, and Jackson became known thereafter as Stonewall.

In the spring of 1862, Jackson maintained a bold campaign against Union forces in the Shenandoah Valley. His recipe for success was to "mystify, mislead and surprise the enemy."[8] With only 16,000 men, Jackson dogged a Union army of 64,000, fighting and winning five battles along the way. Jackson's "foot cavalry" marched 676 miles (108 km) in 48 days.[9]

On May 2, 1863, during the Battle of Chancellorsville, Jackson was hit by friendly fire. Doctors amputated his left arm, and Jackson subsequently contracted pneumonia. When General Lee heard Jackson was dying, he said, "He has lost his left arm, but I have lost my right arm."[10]

The Battle of Antietam was a bloodbath. Lee entered the thick of the battle to rally his men, but at the end of the day, the rebels were forced to retreat across the Potomac. No ground had been gained by either side, and more than 20,000 men lay dead or wounded.[11]

Lee had not achieved the decisive victory he had envisioned. Some Confederate officers criticized Lee's decision to divide his forces, believing if he had concentrated his troops in one area, McClellan would not have been able to force a retreat. The soldiers were demoralized following Antietam. Adding insult to injury, Maryland had not welcomed the Confederate army with open arms; in fact, the invasion solidified the state's desire to fight for the North. President Lincoln claimed Antietam as a victory for the Union, and he used the occasion to announce that the Emancipation Proclamation would go into effect on January 1, 1863. With that declaration, the South lost any chance of getting assistance from the antislavery United Kingdom.

ANGEL OF THE BATTLEFIELD

Clara Barton, a clerk at the US Patent Office in Washington, DC, was present at some of the bloodiest conflicts of the war, including Antietam. When the war started in 1861, Barton saw that supplies and organization were needed to feed and treat wounded soldiers. She lobbied the army to let her bring supplies to the front. At Antietam, she worked so close to the front lines that a musket ball passed under her arm, killing the soldier she tended. Following the war, Barton took on the task of identifying the war dead, and she also founded the American Red Cross.

Lee still believed that to win the war he must strike a devastating blow to the Union army. Conquering territory was not the goal; instead he sought to convince Northerners the human cost of preserving the Union would be too high a price to pay. So, in 1863, Lee once again invaded the North. The little town of Gettysburg, Pennsylvania, would become the turning point of the Civil War and the place where Robert E. Lee would prove he was not invincible.

FAILURE AT GETTYSBURG

The Battle of Gettysburg began on July 1 with a skirmish between Confederate divisions and Union cavalry on the rolling fields north of town. At the end of the

Most fighting at Gettysburg took place outside of town, but there was one civilian casualty when the battle took to the streets.

day, Union troops retreated to Culp's Hill and Cemetery Hill, two places of high ground that gave them a defensive advantage.

By the next morning, 65,000 Confederates and 85,000 Union soldiers had amassed for battle.[12] The Union front was shaped like a fishhook, with Culp's and Cemetery Hills on the right, and Big Round Top and Little Round Top on the left. On the second day, Lee attacked the entire line and almost broke through; however, when dusk fell, the high ground remained in Union hands.

Then Lee made a fateful decision. He asserted that one more assault on the Union center would force the enemy to retreat. General James Longstreet tried to convince the general such a charge was suicide, but Lee was determined. "The enemy is there," he said, pointing toward Cemetery Ridge, "and I am going to strike him."[13]

At 1:00 p.m. on July 3, in an assault later known as "Pickett's Charge," General George Pickett led 15,000 rebels across the field toward the Union center on Cemetery Ridge. The troops were slaughtered as thousands of bullets and cannonballs mowed them down. As the survivors fled back to the woods, General Lee rode out to meet them. He told a despondent General Pickett, "This has been my fight and upon my shoulders rests the blame."[14]

The next day, Lee's troops slipped south of the Potomac as Union soldiers spent Independence Day burying the dead and tending to the wounded.

In contrast to Lee finishing second in his class at West Point in 1829, Pickett finished dead last in the class of 1846. Pickett advanced through the ranks to major general by the time of his ill-fated role in the Battle of Gettysburg.

Approximately 3,150 Union soldiers and 4,000 Confederate soldiers lost their lives at Gettysburg. Lee would never again invade the North.[15]

Gettysburg crippled the Confederate army over the long term. All told, nearly 28,000 Confederate soldiers were killed, wounded, captured, or missing in action.[16] The South had no way to replace the dead or permanently injured soldiers. For the rest of the war, Lee would fight in a defensive posture until he finally surrendered.

General Grant, *seated third from left*, gained the respect of President Lincoln because he made do with the resources and troops available to him.

CHAPTER
★ 5 ★

UNCONDITIONAL SURRENDER GRANT

In the predawn hours of April 7, 1862, Major General Ulysses S. Grant took shelter under a tree. The previous day, Confederates had launched a surprise attack against Union forces encamped on the banks of the Tennessee River. When night fell, the Confederates held the upper hand. Now, as rain poured down over the brim of Grant's hat, the cries from the wounded mingled with the drumbeat of the downpour. Brigadier General William Tecumseh Sherman approached his commanding officer. "Well, Grant," Sherman said, "we've had the devil's own day of it, haven't we?" On a day when his army had suffered 7,000 casualties, Grant's response revealed the calm, determined character of the man who would lead the Union to victory. "Yes," Grant replied, "Lick 'em tomorrow, though."[1]

IMPROBABLE LEADER

Hiram Ulysses Grant was born in Point Pleasant, Ohio, on April 27, 1822. Concerned his son lacked ambition, Grant's father insisted he attend West Point. When Grant arrived at the academy, he discovered the school had registered him as Ulysses S. Grant. Rather than make a fuss, he adopted the new name. Grant was downgraded for sloppy dress and tardiness, and he graduated twenty-first in a class of thirty-nine. Following graduation, he joined the infantry and was stationed outside of Saint Louis, Missouri, where he eventually met and married Julia Dent.

Grant had his first battle experience in the Mexican–American War, a conflict he bitterly but quietly opposed. He believed his first duty was to his country and was commended for his bravery on the battlefield. After the war, Grant was stationed in California. There, he began to drink—too much and too often. Grant was in charge of paying the troops, and in 1854, he was caught dispensing money while intoxicated. He was given a choice: be tried by a military court or resign. Grant resigned.

As a civilian, Grant struggled to support his family, so when Lincoln called for volunteers after Fort Sumter, Grant immediately reenlisted. He was promoted

Although Grant was a soldier to the core, he detested war and felt it was to be avoided at all costs.

to brigadier general in August 1861, and the following winter he earned a name for himself by capturing Fort Henry and Fort Donelson in Tennessee. When Confederate general Simon Bolivar Buckner, the defender of Fort Donelson, requested a meeting with Grant to discuss terms of surrender, Grant's reply was clear: "No terms except an unconditional and immediate surrender can be accepted."[2] Making a wordplay on Grant's adopted initials, newspapers hailed him as "Unconditional Surrender Grant," and he became a national hero.[3]

The public's affection for Grant was short-lived, however, as Grant's leadership was questioned just a few months later following the Battle of Shiloh. He forced a rebel retreat on the second day of battle, but the casualty rate appalled the nation: of the 100,000 men from both sides who fought at Shiloh, nearly one-fourth were killed or wounded.[4] Rumors spread that Grant had been drunk when the Union was attacked. Lincoln was urged to remove Grant from command, but he refused, saying, "I can't lose this man. He fights."[5] Nonetheless, Grant's field army was taken over by General Henry Halleck, and Grant was demoted to Halleck's assistant. Grant's fortunes changed again just a few weeks later when Lincoln recalled General Halleck to Washington, and Grant was put back in charge.

Soon Grant redeemed himself with a key victory in the West. Lincoln's Anaconda strategy depended on seizing control of the Mississippi River. This required the capture of Vicksburg, Mississippi, a city that sat high on the river bluffs. Throughout the spring of 1863, Grant tried everything to break through the city's defenses. He even dug canals and blew up levees, but every method failed. So Grant devised a bold plan. With the help of steamboats and gunboats,

In 1866, the US War Department established a cemetery to bury the remains of soldiers who died at the Battle of Shiloh. Both sides sustained huge casualties during this battle, and General Grant was criticized by many in the North for being caught off guard.

he ferried his army across the Mississippi River into the heart of Confederate territory. Cut off from communications and supplies, Grant approached Vicksburg from the rear while General Sherman attacked the city from the front.

AFRICAN-AMERICAN SOLDIERS

African Americans made up approximately 1 percent of the North's population, but black men comprised fully 10 percent of the Union army.[6] Most of these men were former slaves from the South. Approximately 179,000 African Americans fought for the Union army and 19,000 for the navy by war's end.[7] Despite the heroism and bravery they displayed on many battlefields, these troops were often assigned menial tasks. Their officers were almost always white, and they were paid three dollars less per month than white soldiers until 1864, when equal pay was enacted. Black soldiers in the Union army who were captured by the Confederate army met a grim fate, as it was the official policy of the Confederate Congress to execute black prisoners of war. In instances where they were not executed, they were frequently subjected to forced labor by their Confederate captors.

After fighting several battles on the way, Grant had Vicksburg in a vice. Then he squeezed.

Union guns pounded the city by land while navy gunboats battered it from the river. Vicksburg's citizens took shelter in snake-filled caves dug into hillsides. Disease spread quickly, and food ran low. Finally, on July 3, the same day that Union troops achieved victory at Gettysburg, white flags rose along the Confederate line. Hungry rebels marched out of the city and surrendered their weapons. Grant occupied the city on July 4, 1863—Independence Day.

President Lincoln was overjoyed. He had finally found a general who could deliver a decisive victory. The day after Vicksburg surrendered, Lincoln said,

"Grant is my man, and I am his, for the rest of the war."[8] By March 1864, Lincoln had promoted Grant to general-in-chief. As head of all Union armies, Grant was in charge of war strategy.

The generals who had preceded Grant all believed victory lay in the capture of Richmond. Grant knew better. Victory would only come when Robert E. Lee and the Army of Northern Virginia were defeated.

OUT OF THE WILDERNESS TO VICTORY

Spring flowers turned blood red when General Grant and General Lee finally met on a Virginia battlefield in May 1864. Grant led his army across the Rapidan River into a stretch of dark woods known as the Wilderness. His aim was to get between Lee's army and Richmond. However, Lee anticipated Grant's move and attacked when federal troops were still in the middle of the dense, almost impenetrable forest. For two brutal days the fighting raged. Gunpowder turned

ON THE MENU IN VICKSBURG

As the siege of Vicksburg dragged on, people began starving. One resident created a menu for a fictitious restaurant in which every dish featured mule. People ate horse meat, dog meat, and bread concocted from corn and dried peas. Oxen killed by enemy shells were sold in butcher shops alongside rats. On June 28, 1863, Confederate general John Pemberton received a letter from his troops advising that if he could not feed them, he had better surrender, because the army was ready to mutiny. Pemberton surrendered.

GRANT'S ORDER NO. 11

General Grant disagreed with the Treasury Department's policy of allowing Northern cotton traders, some of them Jewish, to travel to the front lines and purchase cotton from Southern planters. In November 1862, he barred all cotton merchants, specifically "Israelites," from traveling through the western district he controlled. When traders violated the order, Grant gave all "cotton speculators, Jews, and other vagrants" 24 hours to leave the region or he would send them to the battlefront.[10] A few weeks later, Grant issued Order No. 11. This expelled all Jews, not just cotton traders, from Tennessee. President Lincoln ordered Grant to revoke the order. In his later years, Grant apologized for the order as an inappropriate means of undercutting the black market for cotton. During his presidency, he appointed more Jews to public office than any of his predecessors.

the woodlands into a sulfurous cauldron. Brush caught fire and burned many wounded men alive.

Despite the casualties, Grant did not retreat. General Lee might have struck fear in the hearts of previous Union generals, but Grant would not be cowed. When one of his officers described how Lee was certain to outflank the Union army, Grant rose, removed the cigar from his mouth, and loudly proclaimed that he was "heartily tired of hearing what Lee is going to do. . . . Go back to your command, and try to think what we are going to do ourselves."[9]

When the Battle of the Wilderness ended on May 7, 1864, Union soldiers were ordered to march. They were convinced they were retreating to

Washington, DC, as they had done under so many previous commanders. But when the army reached a crossroads, officers ordered the troops to turn south—toward Richmond. "On to Richmond," the men cried.[11] Suddenly, General Grant appeared on horseback. The troops cheered and tossed their hats, glad for a leader who was prepared to fight hard to end the war.

For six long weeks, Grant and Lee tried to crush each other. After the Wilderness came the battles of Spotsylvania and Cold Harbor. Then the Union army reached Petersburg, Virginia, and settled in for a ten-month siege.

As the months rolled on, the Confederate line around Petersburg thinned as the Union line grew thicker.

GRANT THE BEAR CATCHER

When the siege of Petersburg dragged on under Grant's leadership through the summer of 1864, Northerners feared the war would never end. However, that fall, General Sherman led the army on a march through Georgia, capturing the entire state. When Lincoln got the news that Georgia was in federal hands, he bragged, "Grant has the bear by the hind leg while Sherman takes off its hide."[12]

Lee tried to break out of Petersburg, but Grant mounted a massive assault on April 2, 1865. As Union troops poured into the city, Lee's army slipped away toward Appomattox, Virginia. Lee gave the order to evacuate Richmond as he retreated to the southwest. Grant followed. The men would soon meet face to face.

James Longstreet, *standing third from left*, did not support secession, but he believed in states' rights and declared his allegiance to the Confederacy.

GREAT ROCK COMMANDER: JAMES LONGSTREET

General James Longstreet feared his commander was about to make a fatal mistake. It was July 3, 1863, and after two days of fighting, Union forces remained entrenched on hills around Gettysburg, Pennsylvania. General Robert E. Lee was convinced one strong charge into the center of the Union line would break the enemy. Longstreet disagreed. He later recalled telling Lee, "I have been a soldier all my life. . . . It is my opinion that no 15,000 men ever arranged for battle can take that position."[1] But Lee did not listen. The Battle of Gettysburg not only changed the outcome of the war; it also cemented—for the worse—the historical reputation of James Longstreet.

A MILITARY MAN

Longstreet was born into a middle-class family in South Carolina on January 8, 1821. At West Point, he found academics difficult, preferring activities such as horsemanship, sword fighting, and sports. Longstreet graduated in 1842, fifty-fourth in a class of fifty-six.

The Mexican–American War was Longstreet's training ground. When the Eighth Infantry stormed the Chapultepec fortress in Mexico City, Longstreet carried the flag and was shot in the leg. This experience taught Longstreet the dangers of a frontal assault, a lesson that hit home at Gettysburg years later.

When the Civil War began, Longstreet joined the Confederate army as a brigadier general. At the First Battle of Bull Run, his courage and calm under fire earned him praise, so he was promoted to major general and given command of a division.

Longstreet forged his relationship with Robert E. Lee during the Seven Days Battle. In this series of battles to halt McClellan's advance up the Virginia Peninsula, Longstreet stood out as Lee's most reliable general. At the Second Battle of Bull Run, he displayed his deliberate yet bold style of leadership. Reluctant to throw his men into a battle without proper preparations, Longstreet personally studied the terrain and convinced Lee to postpone his planned assault until they found a better approach. Then the situation changed when Union General John Pope attacked Stonewall Jackson's men. Longstreet spotted a weak spot in the Union line and seized the opportunity. More than 25,000 Confederate soldiers charged toward the federal troops, regimental flag bearers leading each line.[2] For four hours, Longstreet's division pounded the Union, and the Confederates emerged victorious.

COMRADES IN ARMS

General Lee often relied on Longstreet's advice, referring to him fondly as "My Old War Horse."[3] At the Battle of Gaines' Mill, Longstreet commanded two brigades and attacked a wall of Union soldiers. As the Union line exploded in fire and smoke, the rebels drove forward in a wave. They shot, clubbed, and bayonetted their way through to seize 14 Union cannons. One officer compared Longstreet to a rock, given his steadiness in the face of chaos. Lee described Longstreet as "the staff in my right hand."[4]

Longstreet was not afraid to take risks as long as there was a chance of success, but he would not endanger his men unnecessarily. Concern for his troops pushed Longstreet to challenge Lee on the third day of the Battle of Gettysburg.

STRATEGIC CALAMITY

Longstreet and Lee differed on the key strategy for the war. Longstreet believed more troops should be sent to Tennessee and Mississippi, while Lee

believed the key to the war was in the East, and he wanted a large raid into Northern territory.

On July 1, 1863, as General Meade's federal troops were entrenched on the hills and ridges to the south and east of Gettysburg, Longstreet and Lee stood on Seminary Ridge surveying the Union position. Longstreet believed a Confederate attack was ill-advised in light of the strong Union position. He told Lee they should move around the Northern army, getting between it and Washington, DC. Once they secured a defensible position, they would essentially force General Meade to come to them. Lee

Lieutenant General Longstreet's leadership on several battlefields gained him the respect and admiration of General Lee.

jabbed a fist in the direction of the Union troops and said, "If the enemy is there tomorrow, we must attack him."[5]

The morning of the second day dawned, and Longstreet once again voiced his objections to launching an assault. Once again Lee rejected the advice. He ordered Longstreet to march his men around the Union flank and then attack northward, up Cemetery Ridge to the enemy line. Longstreet reluctantly complied, but to avoid detection, he had to change his route at the last minute. This caused his divisions to begin their advance hours later than Lee had expected.

Longstreet's First Corps was known as the "great rock."[6] At 4:00 p.m. on July 2, that rock rolled forward. Union artillery roared through the woods and across the field. One man said, "I could hear bones crash like glass in a hail storm."[7] Longstreet's troops marched toward a wall of musket fire and death. When his men saw Longstreet riding among them, they cheered. He shouted, "Cheer less, men, and fight more."[8] After about three hours, Longstreet and his troops drove Union forces out of the Peach Orchard and secured that key position. When the fighting subsided, his greatly depleted ranks bedded down on the blood-soaked ground. During the same afternoon, intense battles had been waged at nearby Devil's Den and Little Round Top, with mixed results for the two armies.

LEE'S EYES AND EARS

In a war fought without radio or telephones, the cavalry provided intelligence about the opposing army, and cavalry commander James Ewell Brown Stuart, known as Jeb, did so for General Lee. In his scarlet-lined cape and feather-plumed hat, Stuart was a flamboyant and daring leader. In June 1862, he led 1,200 cavalry on a mission to learn the position of General McClellan's troops.

On this "ride around McClellan," Stuart circumnavigated the entire Union army in three days.[10] However, during the Battle of Gettysburg, Stuart lost contact with Lee's army. He did not return until the second day of the battle, too late to provide intelligence information that would have helped General Lee. Lee went into battle lacking essential details about the Union forces' movements.

The third day of battle dawned, and Longstreet was still unable to convince Lee to change his strategy. At 1:00 p.m. on July 3, General Lee ordered Longstreet to charge the center of the Union line on Cemetery Ridge. Longstreet complied with great reluctance, telling his artillery officer, "I don't want to make this attack. I believe it will fail . . . I would not make it even now, but that General Lee has ordered it and expects it."[9] Before the charge was launched, Confederate and Union artillery lobbed shells at each other. Longstreet bravely rode up and down his line, heedless of the explosions around him.

The artillery barrage ended. General George Pickett, commander of the division that would lead the charge, asked Longstreet if it was time to begin. Longstreet could not speak the words that would send his men into what he

Lieutenant General Longstreet, *standing*, strongly disagreed with General Lee's decision to make a frontal assault on the Union army at Gettysburg. He was overcome with emotion when Major General Pickett asked if it was time to advance.

was certain would be a slaughter. He was silent for a long moment, and then he just nodded.

"Pickett's Charge" was a complete disaster for the rebel troops. Approximately half of the attack force was killed, wounded, or captured. The Confederates

WOMEN OF GETTYSBURG

Hundreds of female nurses tended the wounded at Gettysburg. Twenty-three-year-old Cornelia Hancock nursed scores of men who lay packed on boards stretched across the pews inside a church. Her memoirs describe the lack of doctors, the stench of the unburied dead, and the "sea of anguish" in which she worked.[11] Helen Gilson single-handedly cared for 250 Confederate wounded when the hospital she worked in was cut off from the main camp by a flooded stream.[12] Annie Etheridge wore a Union uniform and rode along the front, directing the removal of the wounded. She served in at least 32 battles and eventually was awarded the Kearny Cross, a Union combat medal recognizing "overwhelming bravery."[13]

withdrew, bringing the Battle of Gettysburg to an end. Rain fell the next day, July 4, as the Confederates retreated south. General Lee had lost one-third of his army. In a letter written shortly after the battle, Longstreet said he wished all the blame would fall on his shoulders, because General Lee needed all the support his subordinates could give him. Longstreet did not know then that after the war ended, he would indeed become the scapegoat for the Confederate defeat at Gettysburg.

GEORGE MEADE

1815–1872

On June 28, 1863, General George Meade was awakened in his tent by a messenger from the War Department. The Confederate Army of Northern Virginia had advanced into Maryland, and Meade was ordered to take full command of the Union army. He said, "I've been tried and condemned without a hearing, and I suppose I shall have to go to the execution."[14] General Joe Hooker, whom Meade was replacing following Hooker's decisive defeat at Chancellorsville, had left no battle plans. Meade quickly began marching his troops toward Pennsylvania while also positioning the army to shield Washington, DC. Although Meade would be credited with defeating the Confederates at Gettysburg, Lincoln and others faulted him for failing to pursue the wounded Confederate army as it retreated to Virginia—a strategy that many historians believe would have ended the war. In March 1864, Meade's reputation for caution led President Lincoln to replace him with Ulysses S. Grant as commander of all Union forces.

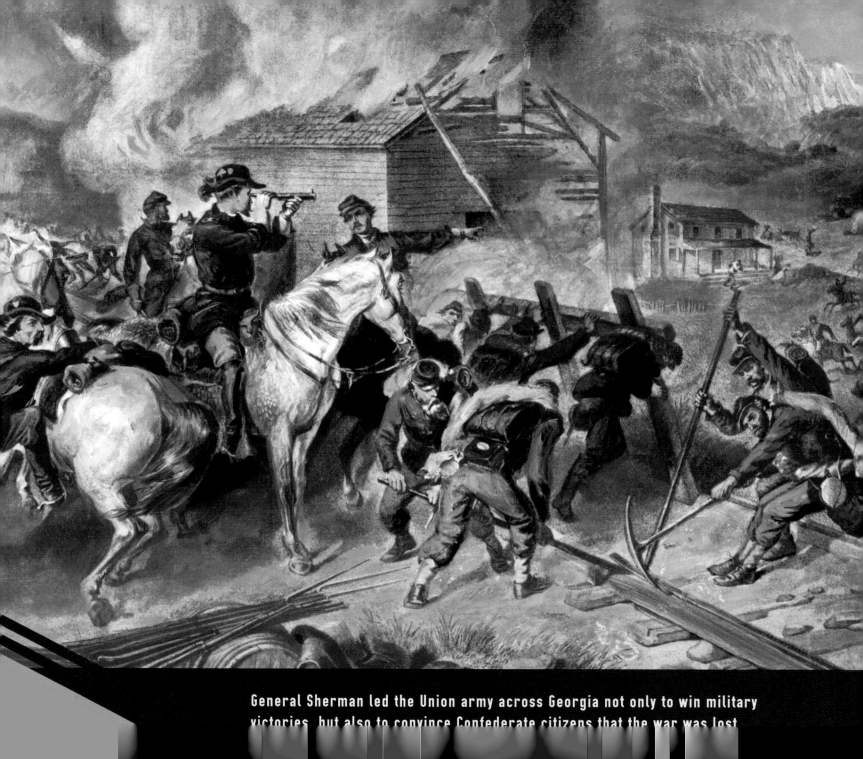

General Sherman led the Union army across Georgia not only to win military
victories, but also to convince Confederate citizens that the war was lost.

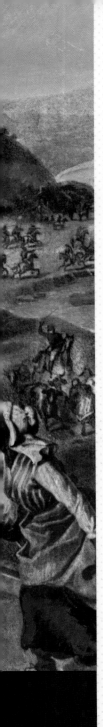

TOTAL WAR: WILLIAM TECUMSEH SHERMAN

In April 1864, Union general William Tecumseh Sherman stood on top of Lookout Mountain, Tennessee. Northern Georgia stretched before him. An endless canopy of trees topped the rugged land, and brown rivers snaked through deep valleys. The one clear path that cut through this thick wilderness was the Western and Atlantic Railroad. Sherman decided to follow that single track and carve a swath of destruction from Atlanta to Savannah that would "make Georgia howl."[1]

MADMAN AND FREAK

William Tecumseh Sherman was born on February 8, 1820, in Lancaster, Ohio. His father, a successful lawyer and judge, chose Tecumseh as the middle name of his sixth child to honor the Shawnee leader of a Native American rebellion in 1812. William Sherman's friends and family fondly called him "Cump" throughout his life.[2]

Judge Sherman died when William was young, leaving William's mother with 11 children to raise and no inheritance. The family of the Shermans' neighbor and friend, Senator Thomas Ewing, raised William. He attended West Point, graduating sixth in the class of 1840. William resigned from the army in 1853 and worked in banking and law before becoming superintendent of the Louisiana Military Academy in 1859. When the Civil War broke out, he left Louisiana and rejoined the US Army. Although he had lived in the South for many years and admired Southern culture, he wanted to remain loyal to the US Constitution "as long as a fragment of it survives."[3]

Unlike other leaders, Sherman was convinced from the start that the war would be long and bloody. His first command at the First Battle of Bull Run on July 21, 1861, reinforced this view. Sherman's soldiers were unruly and poorly trained volunteers. During the battle, they ignored their commander's orders

After a 13-year career in the army, Sherman resigned to be a banker in San Francisco, California, during the gold rush. His brother, a US senator, secured him an appointment as colonel in the Union army when the Civil War began.

and fled to the rear of the fighting. Sherman felt "absolutely disgraced" as a commander and wanted to "sneak into some quiet corner."[4]

Military officials, on the other hand, were impressed with Sherman's leadership. In August 1861, he was promoted to brigadier general. The First Battle of Bull Run taught Sherman the Union army desperately needed discipline and training. He set himself to that task so diligently his soldiers loathed him. On one occasion, a New York captain told Sherman his three-month enlistment was up and he was heading home. Sherman reached for his pistol and told the soldier, "If you attempt to leave without orders . . . I will shoot you like a dog."[5]

Sherman was assigned to command troops in Kentucky, a state that had remained in the Union but included a substantial minority in favor of secession. General Albert Sidney Johnston and 13,000 Confederates occupied lower parts of the state. Sherman's leadership position worried him. He was the senior officer charged with holding the thin line that separated North and South. One mistake could flip Kentucky into the Confederacy. Sherman became almost paralyzed as he inflated the size of Johnston's army in his imagination. He stopped eating and sleeping. He chain-smoked as he wrote one letter after another to officials explaining how formidable Johnston's forces were. In October 1861, Sherman met with Secretary of War Benjamin Cameron and explained he could not attack Johnston's army until he had at least 60,000 troops, with an eventual goal of having 200,000.[6] Cameron was stunned. A reporter present at the meeting later published Sherman's statements in the *New York Tribune*. Other news outlets picked up the story, and Sherman was characterized as unfit for duty and called a madman and a freak.

Although hurt by these characterizations, Sherman also feared for his own mind. He wrote to his wife, "The idea of going down to History with a fame such as threatens me nearly makes me crazy, indeed I may be so now."[7] Ellen Sherman went to Kentucky and found her husband in a "morbid state of anxiety."[8] General Henry Halleck put Sherman on a 20-day leave. Sherman contemplated suicide, but he felt taking his own life would disgrace his family.

REPUTATION REDEEMED

Sherman remained in the army, and in April 1862 he redeemed himself at the Battle of Shiloh. Early in the battle, Sherman was so close to the fighting that his orderly was killed, and Sherman's right hand was slashed open by buckshot. He rode among his men, heedless of the bullets, quietly giving orders. Grant sent a messenger to ask how Sherman was doing. Sherman replied, "Tell Grant if he has any men to spare I can use them; if not, I will do the best I can."[9] And he did. Sherman's leadership on the first day of the Battle of Shiloh held the Confederates off until reinforcements could arrive.

SHERMAN CONVINCED GRANT TO STAY

Criticism of General Grant's leadership during the April 1862 Battle of Shiloh, which resulted in a large number of Union casualties, almost led him to resign from the army. Grant was packing his bags when Sherman stopped by his tent. He reminded Grant that he, too, had been ridiculed and criticized publicly, but Shiloh had given him a second chance to prove himself. Sherman urged Grant not to resign because "some happy accident might restore [you] to favor and [your] true place."[10] Grant did not resign, and the following summer he captured Vicksburg and changed the course of the war.

SHERMAN'S RACISM

When African Americans began serving as soldiers, Sherman balked. In April 1863, he wrote to his wife that he would "prefer to have this a white man's war."[12] When he was told he must comply with efforts to recruit black troops, Sherman told his troops that anyone who tried to enlist black laborers as soldiers would be arrested. On July 18, 1864, President Lincoln ordered Sherman to comply with the recruitment law, but Sherman found ways to block black men from joining his army for the duration of the war.

A friendship formed between Grant and Sherman during this battle that influenced the rest of the war. Grant later wrote that although Sherman's troops were inexperienced in combat, he believed that "their commander, by his constant presence . . . inspired a confidence in officers and men that enabled them to render services on that bloody battlefield worthy of the best of veterans."[11] After the battle, Sherman was promoted to major general. In 1864, when Grant was appointed commander in chief of the Union army, he assigned Sherman a key role that would hasten the end of the war. While Grant attacked the Army of Northern Virginia, Sherman would strike General Joseph Johnston's army in Georgia. The pair maintained relentless pressure on the Confederates until they surrendered.

DRIVING A STAKE THROUGH THE SOUTH

In the fall of 1863, Sherman wrote to Grant that compromise with the South was impossible. "I would make this war as severe as possible," he wrote, "and show no symptoms of tiring till the South begs for mercy."[13] This statement defined Sherman's concept of total warfare. He intended to take the war to the doorsteps of Confederate citizens and make them pay for seceding.

In May 1864, Sherman led 100,000 troops out of Chattanooga, Tennessee, into Georgia, pushing Johnston's army toward Atlanta. President Jefferson Davis, convinced that Johnston would surrender Atlanta, replaced him with General John Bell Hood on July 17. By the end of August, however, Hood's defenses collapsed and the rebels fled the city, burning it as they left. On September 2, Sherman's troops took control of the city, prompting him to send a message to Washington, DC, the next day saying, "Atlanta is ours, and fairly won."[14] This victory ensured Lincoln's reelection in November. Grant praised Sherman's accomplishments and then told him to quickly begin another campaign. He wanted to keep pressure on the enemy.

Sherman proposed to lead his army southeast from Atlanta to the port city of Savannah. During this 225-mile (362 km) march, the men would forage for food along the way, living off the crops and livestock of Georgia. In addition to seeking military victory, his objective was to break the will of Southerners and destroy their capacity to continue the war. Grant and Lincoln were skeptical of Sherman's strategy. If Sherman did not destroy John Bell Hood's army, Hood could move up through Tennessee and Kentucky and into Ohio.

The stakes were huge. One wrong move could lengthen the war even further. Grant made a leap of faith and authorized the plan. Sherman intentionally cut all railroad and telegraph connections to the North, reasoning that by not having to guard supply or communication lines, all of his troops would be available to engage on the battlefield. On November 16, 1864, his army left Atlanta. They marched in four columns across a front 60 miles (97 km) wide. Per Sherman's orders, an elite group of foragers, known as "bummers," moved ahead of the huge army.[15] They confiscated vegetables, livestock, and horse feed. The soldiers pried up railroad tracks, heated them red-hot, and twisted them around trees, destroying Georgia's rail system. Thousands of slaves hailed the army as liberators and joined the march.

In early December, Sherman neared Savannah and reestablished contact with the North. Sherman learned Grant was bogged down in Petersburg and needed assistance. Sherman quickly closed in on Savannah, and on December 22, 1864, he sent a letter to Lincoln that read: "I beg to present you as a Christmas gift the City of Savannah."[16]

UNCLE BILLY ON THE MARCH

Sherman often marched alongside his men. He would talk nonstop as he walked, hands in his pockets and a black hat pulled low on his forehead. Sherman bathed in rivers with his soldiers and circulated through camp at night dressed in red long underwear and a ratty bathrobe. The troops loved their "Uncle Billy." One poor-spelling private wrote, "I am an awful Cow hart [sic] you know But I shall Die before I will leave as true a Solger [sic] as Billie Sherman."[17]

On December 13, 1864, General Sherman's troops stormed Fort McAllister south of Savannah and captured it in just 15 minutes. Union troops removed ammunition from the fort following the attack.

The North was euphoric. The news even reached Europe, where Sherman was widely hailed as a great military leader. Southerners were devastated. If they could not stop an army marching right through their midst, what hope did they have of winning the war? History would remember Sherman as the master of the strategy of total war.

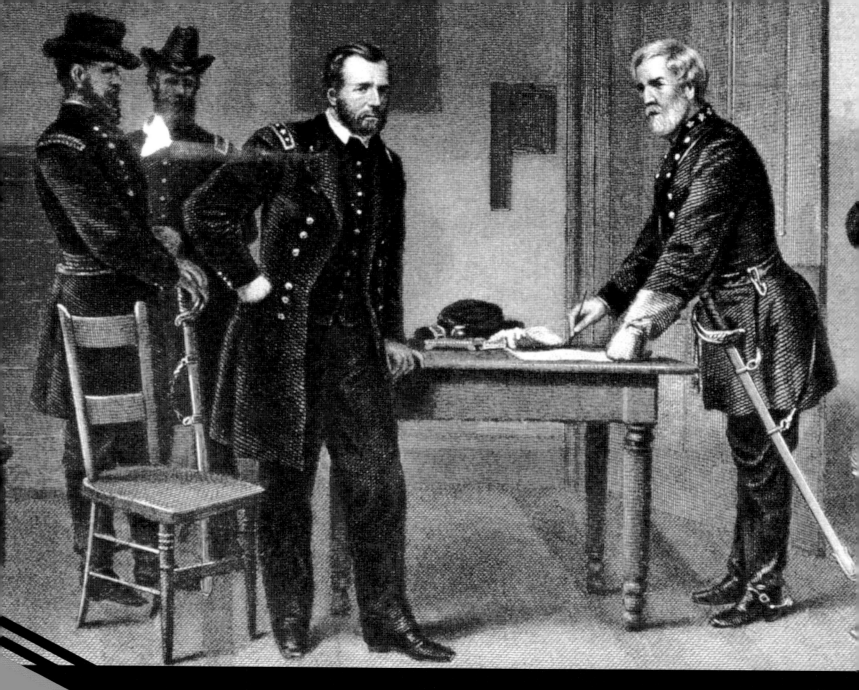

With profound sorrow for the great loss of life during the previous four years,
General Grant, *left*, received the surrender of General Lee, *right*.

THE END AND THE AFTERMATH

In the summer of 1861, the Confederates used Wilmer McLean's farm at Manassas as their headquarters. On July 18, a cannonball crashed through the fireplace into McLean's kitchen. McLean decided to move his family to a quieter part of Virginia—the little town of Appomattox Court House. Four years later, in one of history's curious coincidences, General Lee surrendered his army to General Grant in Wilmer McLean's parlor. McLean earned the right to brag that "the war began in my front yard and ended in my front parlor."[1]

Wilmer McLean's home, formerly a tavern, was chosen by a Union officer for the surrender ceremony because it was the most impressive home in the village. It is now a National Historical Park overseen by the National Park Service.

SURRENDER

Following the fall of Richmond, death and desertion shrank Lee's Army of Northern Virginia from 60,000 to 30,000 men. Grant and the Army of the Potomac pushed Lee's troops west and encircled the starving rebels at Appomattox. On the evening of April 8, 1865, General Lee had two choices: break through the line of Union forces or surrender. After provoking a last-ditch attack on General Philip Sheridan's cavalry unit, it was apparent Lee's forces were surrounded by several Union divisions, and victory was impossible. Lee knew he had to meet with Grant to discuss surrender, even though Lee would rather, as he said, "die a thousand deaths."[2]

Lee arrived at the home of Wilmer McLean at 1:00 p.m. on April 9, and Grant showed up 30 minutes later. Grant still wore the mud-splattered private's uniform he had been wearing on his morning ride. Lee, by contrast, had donned a new dress uniform, and a jewel-studded sword hung at his side. Lincoln had authorized Grant to offer a "tender peace" with generous surrender terms.[3] The two generals discussed the terms, Grant wrote them down, and the pair parted.

It was an emotional moment for both leaders. Grant later wrote how depressed he felt. "I felt like anything rather than rejoicing at the downfall of a foe who had fought so long and valiantly, and had suffered so much for a cause, though that cause was, I believe, one of the worst for which a people ever fought."[4] As Lee rode back to his camp, his soldiers lined the road, removed their hats, and bowed their heads. A crowd of soldiers waited outside Lee's tent. He told them it was

SURRENDER TERMS

When Lee surrendered the Army of Northern Virginia, he agreed to the following terms: all officers and enlisted men would be paroled; all Confederate military equipment would be relinquished; Confederate soldiers who owned their own horses could keep them; and Grant would give food rations for 25,000 soldiers to the starving Southern force.[5] As long as the rebels returned to their homes and did not take up arms against the United States, they would be left in peace.

time to go home, and said, "If you make as good citizens as you have soldiers, you will do well, and I shall always be proud of you."[6]

Although there were other Confederate armies throughout the South, Lee's surrender meant that, for all practical purposes, the Civil War was over. When the news reached Washington, DC, fireworks illuminated the sky and a crowd gathered around the White House. President Lincoln made a brief appearance and asked the band to play one of his favorite songs, "Dixie." The popular song that had become the Confederate anthem was once again a tune for all Americans.

CONSPIRACY AND CAPTURE

On Friday, April 14, 1865, Lincoln and his wife headed to Ford's Theatre to watch a comedy called *Our American Cousin*. As the auditorium rang with laughter, actor and Confederate sympathizer John Wilkes Booth slipped into the presidential box and shot Lincoln in the back of the head. Then Booth vaulted over the edge of the box, landing on the stage floor and breaking his leg. Booth hobbled offstage and down an alley, where he escaped on horseback.

President Lincoln was carried to a boardinghouse across the street. Physicians pronounced his wound mortal. As officials and family gathered around Lincoln's bedside, they were shocked to learn other assassins had been at work elsewhere in the city. Secretary of State William H. Seward had been critically wounded by

Booth's accomplice, Lewis Powell. Another coconspirator, George Atzerodt, was supposed to assassinate Vice President Andrew Johnson, but he lost his nerve. Lincoln was pronounced dead at 7:22 a.m. on Saturday, April 15, 1865, just six days after the end of the war that had defined his presidency. As Lincoln drew his last breath, Secretary of War Edwin Stanton sobbed and said to those who were present, "Now he belongs to the ages."[7]

In the days that followed, Lincoln's body traveled by funeral train to Springfield, Illinois, making stops in seven states so grieving citizens could pay their respects. Meanwhile, a manhunt was in full swing for Booth. On April 26,

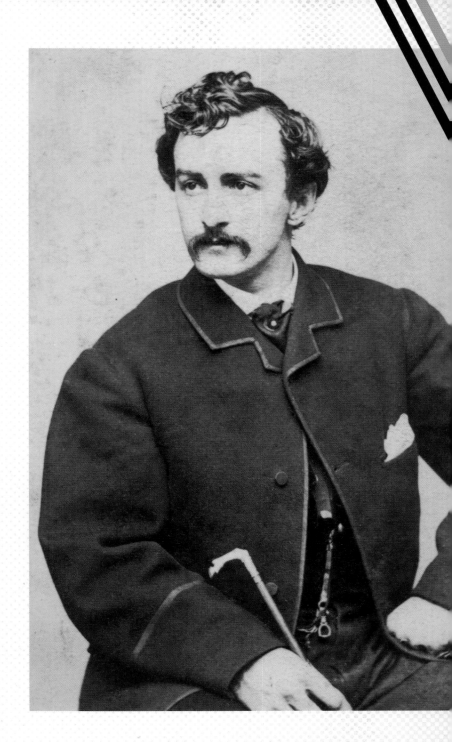

John Wilkes Booth, an ardent defender of slavery, hoped Lincoln's death would rally the Confederacy to keep fighting.

Booth was discovered hiding in a barn in rural Virginia. He resisted capture and was killed. In the frenzy that followed Lincoln's murder, many suspected Southern sympathizers were rounded up and held without trial. Ultimately, seven men and one woman were quickly tried and convicted of conspiracy. Four of them were given life sentences and four were hanged.

Meanwhile, Confederate president Jefferson Davis was on the run. On April 2, General Lee had advised him Richmond could no longer be protected. Davis and his cabinet fled to Danville, Virginia, and upon Lee's surrender, they continued moving south. On May 9, Davis camped with his family and some staff near Irwinville, Georgia. In the predawn hours of May 10, Union lieutenant colonel B. D. Pritchard and more than 100 mounted soldiers surrounded the camp. Davis bolted for his horse, but he was captured a short distance from his tent.

DAVIS IN DRAG

Following the arrest of Jefferson Davis, newspapers across the nation reported he had been dressed in women's clothing when captured. When Secretary of War Stanton received the garments Davis had been wearing, he recognized that Davis's overcoat was designed for males or females, and his "bonnet" was actually a simple black shawl similar to the one President Lincoln sometimes draped over his own shoulders. Stanton did not correct the rumors. He wanted Davis's character to remain damaged in the public eye, and it did.

Jefferson Davis spent two years in federal prison at Fort Monroe, Virginia. He was never tried for treason, nor was any other Confederate leader. Davis was released on bond in 1867.

PRESIDENT JOHNSON VERSUS RADICAL REPUBLICANS

Just hours after President Lincoln died, Vice President Andrew Johnson, a Tennessee Democrat, was sworn in as president of the United States. With Lincoln's sudden death, the task of reconstructing the nation fell to Johnson. His principles and actions put him on a collision course with the Radical Republicans in Congress, who were committed to equal treatment and full voting rights for African Americans.

Johnson had opposed secession, but he also supported states' rights and did not believe in equality for African Americans. Because Congress was not in session when Johnson assumed the presidency, he quickly went about reconstructing the country according to his own vision. Throughout the summer of 1865, it became clear that on Johnson's watch, the economic and political power of whites in the South would be protected at all costs. For example, some Southern states refused to reject secession in their new constitutions. So-called black codes were introduced that severely restricted the rights of former slaves. Former slaves were prohibited from owning land, carrying firearms, or attending public schools in most Southern states.

When Congress reconvened in December 1865, the senators and representatives worked quickly to undo Johnson's pro-Southern actions, and he opposed them every step of the way. On December 6, Johnson's adversaries celebrated the ratification of the Thirteenth Amendment, which prohibited slavery and involuntary servitude within the United States. Congress then defiantly passed the Civil Rights Act of 1866. This law stated that everyone born in the United States (except Native Americans) was a citizen with full constitutional rights. Radical Republicans went even further and passed the Fourteenth Amendment. This amendment defined federal citizenship and extended the full protection of the federal government to all citizens in every state across the nation.

As the 1866 congressional elections loomed, Johnson went on a speaking tour to drum up support for Democratic candidates. His fiery words alienated many voters, and at times he appeared drunk during his speeches. As a result, the election of 1866 put Republicans in control of the House and the Senate. On February 24, 1868, the House voted to impeach Johnson, primarily for dismissing a political opponent, Edwin Stanton, from the president's cabinet in violation of the law. Johnson was acquitted by only one vote.

For the rest of his presidency, Johnson was little more than a figurehead. However, by the end of Reconstruction in 1877, support for the Radical Republican agenda had declined. White Democrats in the South reasserted their power and fostered racial discrimination in many ways. Although African Americans gained many legal and political rights on paper during Reconstruction, it would be close to 100 years before those rights became a reality in everyday life.

FROM TRAITOR TO ICON

After he surrendered, Lee retreated to Richmond. A few days after the war officially ended, he granted an interview that angered Northern audiences. Lee was unapologetic for his role in the national slaughter. He said the North should be lenient with the South, and urged the nation to properly "dispose" of the "negroes."[8] He also asserted that Southerners should not "be judged harshly for contending for that which [they] honestly believed to be right."[9] Lee was never tried for treason. He became the president of Washington College in Lexington, Virginia, and he lived a quiet existence until his death in 1870.

While Lee had learned to accept his defeat at the hands of the Union, other Southern leaders in the 1870s sought to reassert white supremacy in the South. The Lost Cause was a movement of Southerners who sought to do just

NO REPENTANCE

Late in life, Jefferson Davis wrote a lengthy memoir titled *The Rise and Fall of the Confederate Government,* in which he tried to justify Southern secession. Too proud to request a pardon, the former Confederate president never regained his citizenship. Said Davis in 1881, "It has been said that I should apply to the United States for a pardon, but repentance must precede the right of pardon, and I have not repented." Until his death in 1889, he lived as a man without a country.[10]

that. The name derived from Sir Walter Scott's glorified depiction of Scotland's unsuccessful fight for independence from Great Britain in 1745 and 1746. Former Confederates such as Jubal Early led a public relations campaign to recast the Civil War in a positive light, and Lee became the movement's poster boy. Lee was portrayed as a selfless, noble figure who had defended states' rights. Anyone who sullied Lee's memory was denounced. When former Confederate general Longstreet publicly criticized decisions Lee made at Gettysburg, Lost Cause supporters blamed Longstreet for

When the war ended, the trustees of Washington College eagerly invited Lee to be president of the college.

that defeat instead. Longstreet would spend the rest of his life trying to clear his reputation.

The Lost Cause campaign made Lee a national hero, and presidents from Theodore Roosevelt to Dwight D. Eisenhower praised his character and leadership. Statues of Lee, as well as schools named in his honor, still dot the Southern landscape.

CORRUPTION AND CIVIL RIGHTS

Unlike Lee's quiet retreat into private life, Grant remained in the public eye until his death in 1885. Wide public acclaim for his military prowess swept him to victory as the Republican nominee for president in 1868. His inexperience in politics caused him to be a very hands-off president. During his two terms, Grant essentially let Congress have its own way without offering much leadership. Corruption scandals tainted Grant's presidency. While he was not personally involved in these scandals, various schemes implicated his vice president, his secretary of war, and US Treasury staff. Grant's continued popularity propelled him to reelection in 1872, but by the end of his second term, he was well aware of his limitations as chief executive, saying, "It was my fortune, or misfortune, to be called to the office of Chief Executive without previous political training. . . . Mistakes have been made, as all can see, and I admit."[11]

Civil rights was one area where Grant achieved a positive presidential record. The Ku Klux Klan was founded in 1866, with Confederate war hero General Nathan Bedford Forrest serving as one of its early leaders. This terrorist group tried to control African Americans and their white sympathizers through intimidation and violence. Grant used broad executive powers to suspend habeas corpus in parts of the South. When Klan activities continued, Grant sent federal troops into nine counties in South Carolina, and hundreds of suspected terrorists were arrested. Grant's actions crippled the Klan, at least for a time.

Even many Radical Republicans shied away from promoting full voting rights for African Americans, but Grant supported giving black people the vote. The Fifteenth Amendment guaranteed that no male citizen could be barred from voting due to race, color, or status as a former slave. When this amendment was ratified on February 3, 1870, Grant said it was "the most important event that has occurred since the nation came to life."[12] Despite the amendment, Southern states used various methods to deny black people the right to vote, including violence, literacy tests, and poll taxes.

THE LEGACIES OF LEADERSHIP

The Americans who answered the call of leadership during the Civil War did so for multiple reasons. Some were motivated by a sense of duty; others were driven by fear, hatred, or an overarching desire to maintain their way of life. Despite the best intentions with which they entered the fight, these leaders left a mixed legacy. Bravery and blunder stumbled over each other on the battlefield. Strong desires to annihilate the institution of slavery were offset by the vigorous efforts of others to preserve it. What these leaders all shared, however, was an abiding love of country (however they defined country) and hope for a peaceful future.

The Civil War refined and reconfigured the young, growing nation. The federal government asserted its supremacy over the states. The Union, though bruised and tested to the limit, did not break. African Americans were emancipated, at least according to the letter of the law, as the institution of slavery was forever banished from the land. After four dark years of war, the United States remained one people, one nation—indivisible.

THE FIGHT FOR BROADER FREEDOMS

Octavius Catto grew up in Philadelphia, Pennsylvania, home to the nation's largest community of free black people prior to the Civil War. Highly educated, Catto went on to educate others. He taught at the Institute for Colored Youth and founded the Banneker Literary Institute. During the Civil War, Catto became a major in the Union army and organized 11 regiments of black volunteers. He fought to integrate Philadelphia's streetcars, an effort that succeeded in 1867. As the manager and star shortstop of the all-black Pythian Base Ball Club, Catto petitioned for the team to join the National Association, the precursor of today's major league. This effort failed. The ratification of the Fifteenth Amendment gave black men in Philadelphia their first chance to vote in 1871. On his way back from the polls, Catto was shot in the back and killed by a Democratic political opponent. More than 5,000 mourners observed his funeral procession.[13]

TIMELINE

November 6, 1860

Abraham Lincoln is elected president of the United States.

December 20, 1860

South Carolina is the first of 11 states to secede from the United States.

February 18, 1861

Jefferson Davis is inaugurated as president of the Confederate States of America.

April 12, 1861

The Civil War begins with Confederate troops firing on Fort Sumter in Charleston, South Carolina.

August–December 1864

Union general William Sherman marches his army across Georgia.

November 8, 1864

Lincoln is reelected to the presidency.

April 9, 1865

Confederate general Lee surrenders the Army of Northern Virginia.

April 15, 1865

President Lincoln dies from an assassin's bullet.

April 6–7, 1862

The Battle of Shiloh damages the reputation of Union general Ulysses S. Grant.

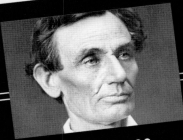

January 1, 1863

President Lincoln signs the Emancipation Proclamation.

July 1–3, 1863

Union general George Meade defeats Confederate general Robert E. Lee in the Battle of Gettysburg.

July 4, 1863

Union general Grant occupies Vicksburg, Mississippi, and gains control of the Mississippi River.

December 6, 1865

The ratification of the Thirteenth Amendment abolishes slavery throughout the United States.

February 24, 1868

The House of Representatives votes to impeach President Andrew Johnson.

July 9, 1868

The ratification of the Fourteenth Amendment defines citizenship and grants equal protection of the law to all citizens.

February 3, 1870

During Grant's presidency, the ratification of the Fifteenth Amendment gives African-American men the right to vote.

ESSENTIAL FACTS

KEY PLAYERS

- President Abraham Lincoln governed the Union.

- President Jefferson Davis governed the Confederacy.

- General Robert E. Lee was the primary commander of the Confederate army.

- General Ulysses S. Grant eventually led the Union army to victory.

- General James Longstreet commanded the First Corps of the Army of Northern Virginia and became the scapegoat for the Confederate loss at Gettysburg after the war.

- General William Tecumseh Sherman led part of the Union army on a march through Georgia, hastening the end of the war.

KEY STATISTICS

- Eleven states seceded from the Union to form the Confederate States of America.

- Following the attack on Fort Sumter, there were fewer than 20,000 soldiers in the entire United States army, yet some 35,000 Union troops took part in the first battle of the war just a few months later.

- The Confederate Congress passed a law that all farms within the Confederacy had to give 10 percent of their produce to the government.

- The bloodiest day in American history occurred at the Battle of Antietam, with more than 20,000 soldiers killed or wounded.

- Nearly 28,000 Confederate soldiers were killed, wounded, captured, or missing in action at the Battle of Gettysburg.

- Union General William Tecumseh Sherman led his troops on a 225-mile (362 km) march from Atlanta to Savannah to destroy the South's will to continue the war.

- Approximately 750,000 soldiers from the Union and Confederate armies lost their lives in the Civil War.

IMPACT ON WAR

Political and military leaders had an immense impact on the nature and duration of the Civil War. Abraham Lincoln, who began the war with the sole objective of reuniting the nation, expanded his goals to include the abolition of slavery throughout the land. Jefferson Davis was a principled, though fairly ineffective, leader of the struggling Confederacy. President Lincoln labored to find a capable military commander until he settled on General Ulysses Grant, while General Robert E. Lee of the Confederacy was widely respected both during and after the war. Other military commanders such as Generals James Longstreet and William Sherman played a pivotal role in shaping the scope and direction of the war.

QUOTE

"If my name ever goes into history it will be for this act, and my whole soul is in it."

—Abraham Lincoln, upon signing the Emancipation Proclamation in 1863

GLOSSARY

AMENDMENT
A formal addition or change to a document.

ARTILLERY
A large gun manned by a crew of operators used to shoot long distances.

CABINET
The president's key advisers.

CAVALRY
A military unit consisting of soldiers mounted on horseback.

CORPS
A large military unit consisting of several infantry divisions, in addition to artillery, cavalry, engineers, and supply units.

DELEGATE
A person sent to a convention to represent a group or a state.

DIVISION
A military unit consisting of two or three infantry brigades.

EMANCIPATION
The act of freeing an individual or group from slavery.

FEDERAL
Relating to, or loyal to, the government of the United States.

IMPEACH
To charge an elected official with wrongdoing.

INAUGURATE
To be formally sworn into public office.

INSTITUTION
An established law or practice in a society.

RATIFY
To formally approve or adopt an idea or document.

SECESSION
The formal withdrawal of one group or region from a political union.

WHITE SUPREMACY
The belief that white people are superior to all other races.

ADDITIONAL RESOURCES

SELECTED BIBLIOGRAPHY

Chadwick, Bruce. *Two American Presidents: A Dual Biography of Abraham Lincoln and Jefferson Davis*. Toronto, ON: Birch Lane, 1999. Print.

Flood, Charles Bracelen. *Grant and Sherman: The Friendship That Won the Civil War*. New York: Farrar, 2005. Print.

Jones, Wilmer L. *Generals in Blue and Gray: Davis's Generals*. Volume II. Westport, CT: Praeger, 2004. Print.

Wert, Jeffry. *General James Longstreet: The Confederacy's Most Controversial Soldier*. New York: Simon, 1993. Print.

FURTHER READINGS

Archer, Jules. *A House Divided: The Lives of Ulysses S. Grant and Robert E. Lee*. New York: Sky Pony, 2015. Print.

Sheinkin, Steve. *Two Miserable Presidents: The Amazing, Terrible, and Totally True Story of the Civil War*. New York: Summer Street, 2008. Print.

Swanson, James. *Chasing Lincoln's Killer*. New York: Scholastic, 2009. Print.

WEBSITES

To learn more about Essential Library of the Civil War, visit **booklinks.abdopublishing.com**. These links are routinely monitored and updated to provide the most current information available.

PLACES TO VISIT

Lincoln Home National Historic Site
426 S. Seventh Street
Springfield, IL 62701
217-492-4241
http://www.nps.gov/liho/index.htm
Visit the home where Abraham Lincoln lived with his wife and children for 17 years. Tour historic sites in the city of Springfield and visit Lincoln's tomb at Oak Ridge Cemetery.

White House & Museum of the Confederacy
(One of three locations of the American Civil War Museum)
1201 E. Clay Street
Richmond, VA 23219
804-649-1861
https://acwm.org
The American Civil War Museum presents the legacy of the Civil War from multiple perspectives: Union and Confederate, enslaved and free African Americans, soldiers and civilians. In addition to the Confederate White House and its nearby museum, exhibits are presented at Historic Tredegar in Richmond and at the Museum of the Confederacy–Appomattox.

SOURCE NOTES

CHAPTER 1. DUELING REPUBLICS

1. "Abraham Lincoln and the Election of 1860." *Abraham Lincoln's Classroom*. The Lehrman Institute, n.d. Web. 15 September 2015.

2. Allen C. Guelzo. *Abraham Lincoln: Redeemer President*. Grand Rapids, MI: Eerdmans, 1999. Print. 245.

3. Geoffrey C. Ward. *The Civil War: An Illustrated History*. New York: Knopf, 1992. Print. 27.

4. Ibid. 29.

5. James M. McPherson. *Tried by War: Abraham Lincoln as Commander in Chief*. New York: Penguin, 2008. Print. 13.

6. Abraham Lincoln. "First Inaugural Address." *Bartleby.com*. n.p., 2 March 1861. Web. 16 Sept. 2015.

7. James McPherson. *Battle Cry of Freedom: The Civil War Era*. New York: Oxford UP, 2003. Print. 273.

8. Geoffrey C. Ward. *The Civil War: An Illustrated History*. New York: Knopf, 1992. Print. 48.

9. Ibid.

10. Steven E. Woodworth and Kenneth J. Winkle. *Atlas of the Civil War*. New York: Oxford UP, 2004. 74. *Google Books*. Web. 2 Jan. 2016.

11. James McPherson. *The War That Forged a Nation: Why the Civil War Still Matters*. New York: Oxford UP, 2015. 54. *Google Books*. Web. 2 Jan. 2016.

12. Geoffrey C. Ward. *The Civil War: An Illustrated History*. New York: Knopf, 1992. Print. 38.

CHAPTER 2. THE GREAT EMANCIPATOR: ABRAHAM LINCOLN

1. Allen C. Guelzo. *Abraham Lincoln: Redeemer President*. Grand Rapids, MI: Eerdmans, 1999. Print. 214.

2. "The United States Army." *Encyclopaedia Britannica*. Encyclopaedia Britannica, n.d. Web. 31 Jan. 2016.

3. Clayton R. Newell and Charles R. Shrader. *Of Duty Well and Faithfully Done: A History of the Regular Army in the Civil War*. Lincoln, Nebraska: U of Nebraska P, 2011. 205. *Google Books*. Web. 2 Jan. 2016.

4. Wilmer L. Jones. *Generals in Blue and Gray: Davis's Generals*. Westport, CT: Praeger, 2004. Print. 105.

5. Bruce Chadwick. *Two American Presidents: A Dual Biography of Abraham Lincoln and Jefferson Davis*. Toronto, ON: Birch Lane, 1999. Print. 244.

6. Geoffrey C. Ward. *The Civil War: An Illustrated History*. New York: Knopf, 1990. Print. 147.

7. Ibid. 242.

8. Allen C. Guelzo. *Abraham Lincoln: Redeemer President*. Grand Rapids, MI: Eerdmans, 1999. Print. 384.

9. Geoffrey C. Ward. *The Civil War: An Illustrated History*. New York: Knopf, 1990. Print. 57.

10. Ibid. 189.

11. "Gettysburg." *Civil War Trust*. Civil War Trust, 2014. Web. 2 Jan. 2016.

12. Geoffrey C. Ward. *The Civil War: An Illustrated History*. New York: Knopf, 1990. Print. 244.

13. Ibid. 166.

14. Ibid.

15. James M. McPherson. *Tried by War: Abraham Lincoln as Commander in Chief*. New York: Penguin, 2008. Print. 157.

16. "Teaching with Documents—The Fight for Equal Rights: Black Soldiers in the Civil War." *National Archives*. The US National Archives and Records Administration, n.d. Web. 2 Jan. 2016.

17. Joel Achenbach. "The Election of 1864 and the Last Temptation of Abraham Lincoln." *Washington Post*. Washington Post, 11 Sept. 2014. Web. 20 Sept. 2015.

18. Robert Wilson. *Mathew Brady: Portraits of a Nation*. New York: Bloomsbury, 2014. 65. *Google Books*. Web. 2 Jan. 2016.

CHAPTER 3. RELENTLESS REBEL: JEFFERSON DAVIS

1. Jefferson Davis. "Jefferson Davis' Farewell Address." *The Papers of Jefferson Davis,* n.p. 2011. Web. 2 Jan. 2016.

2. Ibid.

3. Bruce Chadwick. *Two American Presidents: A Dual Biography of Abraham Lincoln and Jefferson Davis.* Toronto, ON: Birch Lane, 1999. Print. 289.

4. Ibid. 293.

5. Wilmer L. Jones. *Generals in Blue and Gray: Davis's Generals.* Westport, CT: Praeger, 2004. Print. 128.

6. Ibid. 130.

7. "Paper Money in the Civil War." *Learn NC.* UNC School of Education, n.d. Web. 2 Jan. 2016.

8. Julie Golia. "The Emancipation Proclamation: Jefferson Davis Responds." *Brooklyn Historical Society Blog.* Brooklyn Historical Society, 7 Jan. 2014. Web. 22 Sept. 2015.

9. Jefferson Davis. "To the People of the Confederate States of America." *The Papers of Jefferson Davis.* Rice University, 4 April 1865. Web. 24 Sept. 2015.

CHAPTER 4. THE MARBLE MODEL: ROBERT E. LEE

1. Elizabeth Brown Pryor. *Reading the Man: A Portrait of Robert E. Lee through His Private Letters.* New York: Viking, 2007. Print. 291.

2. Ibid. 220.

3. Wilmer L. Jones. *Generals in Blue and Gray: Davis's Generals.* Westport, CT: Praeger, 2004. Print. 74.

4. Elizabeth Brown Pryor. *Reading the Man: A Portrait of Robert E. Lee through His Private Letters.* New York: Viking, 2007. Print. 285.

5. Brian C. Melton. *King of Spades.* Santa Barbara, CA: ABC-CLIO, 2012. 57. *Google Books.* Web. 2 Jan. 2016.

6. Elizabeth Brown Pryor. *Reading the Man: A Portrait of Robert E. Lee through His Private Letters.* New York: Viking, 2007. Print. 322.

7. Wilmer L. Jones. *Generals in Blue and Gray: Davis's Generals.* Westport, CT: Praeger, 2004. Print. 105.

8. Ibid. 107.

9. Ibid.

10. Ibid. 114.

11. "Casualties of Battle." *Antietam.* National Park Service, 12 Dec. 2015. Web. 2 Jan. 2016.

12. Geoffrey C. Ward. *The Civil War: The Complete Text of the Bestselling Narrative History of the Civil War Based on the Celebrated PBS Television Series.* NY: Knopf Doubleday, 2009. Print. 180.

13. Ibid. 186.

14. Wilmer L. Jones. *Generals in Blue and Gray: Davis's Generals.* Westport, CT: Praeger, 2004. Print. 85.

15. "Gettysburg." *Civil War Trust.* Civil War Trust, 2014. Web. 2 Jan. 2016.

16. Ibid.

CHAPTER 5. UNCONDITIONAL SURRENDER GRANT

1. Charles Bracelen Flood. *Grant and Sherman: The Friendship That Won the Civil War.* New York: Farrar, 2005. Print. 3.

2. Ibid. 86.

SOURCE NOTES
CONTINUED

3. Ibid.

4. "Shiloh." *Civil War Trust*. Civil War Trust, 2014. Web. 2 Jan. 2016.

5. Charles Bracelen Flood. *Grant and Sherman: The Friendship That Won the Civil War*. New York: Farrar, 2005. Print. 121.

6. "Teaching with Documents—The Fight for Equal Rights: Black Soldiers in the Civil War." *National Archives*. The US National Archives and Records Administration, n.d. Web. 2 Jan. 2016.

7. Ibid.

8. Charles Bracelen Flood. *Grant and Sherman: The Friendship That Won the Civil War*. New York: Farrar, 2005. Print. 188.

9. Ibid. 243.

10. Edward Longacre. *General Ulysses S. Grant: The Soldier and the Man*. Boston, MA: Da Capo, 2007. 159. *Google Books*. Web. 2 Jan. 2016.

11. Charles Bracelen Flood. *Grant and Sherman: The Friendship That Won the Civil War*. New York: Farrar, 2005. Print. 245-246.

12. Geoffrey C. Ward. *The Civil War: An Illustrated History*. New York: Knopf, 1990. Print. 348.

CHAPTER 6. GREAT ROCK COMMANDER: JAMES LONGSTREET

1. Wilmer L. Jones. *Generals in Blue and Gray: Lincoln's Generals*. Volume I. Westport, CT: Praeger, 2004. Print. 189.

2. Jeffry Wert. *General James Longstreet: The Confederacy's Most Controversial Soldier*. New York: Simon, 1993. Print. 176–177.

3. *The Civil War: A Visual History*. New York: DK, 2011. Print. 186.

4. Jeffry Wert. *General James Longstreet: The Confederacy's Most Controversial Soldier*. New York: Simon, 1993. Print. 152.

5. Ibid. 257.

6. Ibid. 274.

7. Ibid.

8. Ibid. 276.

9. Ibid. 291.

10. Wilmer L. Jones. *Generals in Blue and Gray: Lincoln's Generals*. Volume I. Westport, CT: Praeger, 2004. Print. 203.

11. Cornelia Hancock. *Letters of a Civil War Nurse*. Lincoln, NE: U of Nebraska P, 1971. 4. *Google Books*. Web. 2 Jan. 2016.

12. Pat Leonard. "Nursing the Wounded at Gettysburg." *Opinionator*. New York Times, 7 July 2013. Web. 4 Oct. 2015.

13. Ibid.

14. Wilmer L. Jones. *Generals in Blue and Gray: Lincoln's Generals*. Volume I. Westport, CT: Praeger, 2004. Print. 291.

CHAPTER 7. TOTAL WAR: WILLIAM TECUMSEH SHERMAN

1. Neil Kagan and Stephen Garrison Hyslop. *Eyewitness to the Civil War*. Washington, DC: National Geographic, 2006. 334. *Google Books*. Web. 2 Jan. 2016.

2. Charles Bracelen Flood. *Grant and Sherman: The Friendship That Won the Civil War*. New York: Farrar, 2005. Print. 23.

3. Wilmer L. Jones. *Generals in Blue and Gray: Lincoln's Generals*. Volume I. Westport, CT: Praeger, 2004. Print. 203.

4. Michael Fellman. *Citizen Sherman: A Life of William Tecumseh Sherman*. New York: Random, 1995. Print. 90.

5. Ibid.

6. Charles Royster. *The Destructive War: William Tecumseh Sherman, Stonewall Jackson and the Americans.* New York: Vintage, 1991. Print. 96.

7. Ibid. 98.

8. Ibid. 99.

9. Charles Bracelen Flood. *Grant and Sherman: The Friendship That Won the Civil War.* New York: Farrar, 2005. Print. 107.

10. Ibid. 125.

11. Ibid. 109.

12. Allen C. Guelzo. *Fateful Lightning: A New History of the Civil War and Reconstruction.* New York: Oxford UP, 2012. Print. 236.

13. Charles Royster. *The Destructive War: William Tecumseh Sherman, Stonewall Jackson and the Americans.* New York: Vintage, 1991. Print. 116.

14. "So Atlanta Is Ours and Fairly Won—General Sherman Captures Atlanta." *Chickamauga & Chattanooga.* National Park Service, 4 Jan. 2016. Web. 4 Jan. 2016.

15. Charles Bracelen Flood. *Grant and Sherman: The Friendship That Won the Civil War.* New York: Farrar, 2005. Print. 266.

16. Ibid. 276.

17. Michael Fellman. *Citizen Sherman: A Life of William Tecumseh Sherman.* New York: Random, 1995. Print. 194.

CHAPTER 8. THE END AND THE AFTERMATH

1. Geoffrey C. Ward. *The Civil War: An Illustrated History.* New York: Knopf, 1990. Print. xix.

2. Tamela Baker. "Lee's Last-Ditch Effort." *America's Civil War* 28.1 (2015): 26–33. *Academic Search Premier.* Web. 8 Sept. 2015.

3. Jay Winik. "A Graceful Exit." *American Heritage* 59.4 (2010): 60–61. *Academic Search Premier.* Web. 4 Oct. 2015.

4. Tamela Baker. "Lee's Last-Ditch Effort." *America's Civil War* 28.1 (2015): 26–33. *Academic Search Premier.* Web. 8 Sept. 2015.

5. Eli N. Evans. *Judah P. Benjamin: The Jewish Confederate.* New York: Simon, 1988. 300. *Google Books.* Web. 2 Jan. 2016.

6. Geoffrey C. Ward. *The Civil War: An Illustrated History.* New York: Knopf, 1990. Print. 381.

7. "A Lincoln Commemoration." *Ford's Theatre.* Ford's Theatre, 12 Apr. 2015. Web. 2 Jan. 2016.

8. Elizabeth Brown Pryor. *Reading the Man: A Portrait of Robert E. Lee through His Private Letters.* New York: Viking, 2007. Print. 431.

9. Ibid.

10. Ian Frederick Finseth. *The American Civil War: An Anthology of Essential Writings.* New York: Taylor & Francis, 2006. 539. *Google Books.* Web. 2 Jan. 2016.

11. David Hardin. *After the War: The Lives and Images of Major Civil War Figures After the Shooting Stopped.* Chicago: Dee, 2010. Print. 80.

12. Ibid. 57.

13. Aaron X. Smith. "Murder of Octavius Catto." *The Encyclopedia of Greater Philadelphia.* Encyclopedia of Greater Philadelphia, 2016. Web. 6 January 2016.

INDEX

ABOUT THE AUTHOR

Judy Dodge Cummings is a writer and former history teacher from south central Wisconsin. Some of her other books include *The American Revolution: Experience the Battle for Independence*, *Civil War*, and *Exploring Polar Regions*. Because of his wit, compassion, and courage, Abraham Lincoln is her favorite leader of the Civil War.

ABOUT THE CONSULTANT

Dr. Matt Gallman is a professor at the University of Florida. He has authored books on the Civil War, abolitionist Anna Elizabeth Dickinson, and the Irish famine migration.